SOUL BODIES

by

CHRIS GRISCOM

Published by
The Light Institute Press
Galisteo, New Mexico USA

SOUL BODIES
BY CHRIS GRISCOM

COVER PHOTOS BY LAULA FRITZ AND NAVJIT KANDOLA
EDITING, TYPOGRAPHY, & DESIGN BY SARA BENJAMIN-RHODES

Published by:
The Light Institute Press
HC-75, Box 50
Galisteo, New Mexico 87540 USA

Library of Congress Cataloging-in-Publication Data
Griscom, Chris, 1942-
Soul Bodies / by Chris Griscom.

                 p.   cm.
         ISBN 0-9623696-3-2
         1. Soul.   2. Griscom, Chris, 1942-   3. Light Institute (Galisteo, N.M.)   4. Bodies of man (Occultism)   5. Spiritual life.   6. Spiritual healing   I. Title.
         BP605.L53G753   1996
         299' .93--dc20   96-16027
                                                    CIP

ISBN 0-9623696-3-2, Trade Paperback
Printed in United States of America
Printed with vegetable ink on 100% recycled acid-free paper

DEDICATION

I dedicate this book to the facilitators of The Light Institute, whose Soul Bodies shine so brilliantly out into the world.

OTHER WORKS BY CHRIS GRISCOM ...

BOOKS

The Ageless Body

Feminine Fusion

Healing of Emotion

Ecstasy Is a New Frequency

Time Is an Illusion

Nizhoni: The Higher Self in Education

Ocean Born: Birth as Initiation

Quickening: Meditations for the Millenium

VIDEO TAPES

The Ageless Body

Windows to the Sky, Part One and Two

Death and Samadhi

AUDIO TAPES

The Dance of Relationship/La Danza de las Relaciones

Parent/Child Relationship

Death and Samadhi

Desert Trilogy: Healing, Sexuality, and Radiation

Knowings I & II

The Creative Self

Transcending Adversity

Sense of Abundance

(descriptions of these works are on pages 189-191)

TABLE OF CONTENTS

ACKNOWLEDGMENTS

My greatest admiration to my Divinity students, who reflected with me on the contents of this book and contributed from such wise and illuminated experiences of their own. They are my true Soul Family!

To Navjit Kandola and Laula Fritz, who braved the freezing New Mexico winds with me to bring forth the beautiful images on the covers of this book. You are truly alchemists of beauty and creative expression!

To Sara Benjamin-Rhodes, my editor, my deepest gratitude for your mastery in all aspects of the publication process. It is a great joy to place my book in the hands of such a Being of Light!

My great appreciation to Gregory and Hope and Catherine, whose support carries me through my life with such grace, because of their unfaltering presence and help.

To Teo and Bapu and all of my children who, through their loving patience and wisdom, have helped me to birth this book. Thank You, my Beloveds!

PROLOGUE

I always dreamed the formless. Perhaps we all do.

I could not fathom the infinite wisdom or portent of the fused ovum that produced me. Was there some sweet sound that carried my design to her slippery skin and kissed admittance? Could I ever hope to touch the edge of such an elusive threshold, through which the impregnated void was sucked into the vortex of human existence?

Yet the whisper spoke. It spoke my life and somewhere within me, I answered … yes. Yes, ignite the spark. Prepare the juices. Essence, so singular and all inclusive, begin!

Trembling, the liquid essence imprinted time and scorched itself with rigid form. The past became an unforgiving web bound tightly by conscience and the night.

The future gasped and waited for the present to awaken. Intersecting, they wove a tapestry, to be called my dharma.

So it was cast, and I rushed in to construct a body: A body strong enough to bear the lesson, fluid enough to be transformed, light enough to advance the Soul.

A Soul Body.

Imagine such a thing as a body of the Soul. How could just one body encompass the all of it? No, a thousand bodies couldn't possibly contain it. The Soul must contain the body. Drawing its life's breath, it slips through the veil and composes the sacred ethers into a body of blood and chi.

Where could I find the dimensions for my Soul Body? Must it be male or female? Should it be tall or small? What skin and hair? How would the features describe its character — the story of its purpose and progress, told by each small part?

The forehead and eyes, the nose and ears, hands and thighs — each would tell of predispositions in mind and feelings. Each deep organ, portrayed within the lines and shapes of outer body parts, to define the Soul's intent. What do you choose, Soul? A composition of ancient and close remembrances, orchestrating body movement and style? Will you pluck Roman, Lemurian, African, Asian, Mayan, Indian, galactic, devic, Druid, Greek, or more?

Each new evolutionary thrust is rooted in the soil of lives now spent, where themes transcend and begin. Some themes call love or hate or power. Some teach balance, karma, or cosmic law. The Soul Body selects the themes and packs them into strands that weave the field called Form.

The strands shape the matrix of all possibilities in which magnetic attraction designs points of reference furnished from bodily incarnations in mental, emotional, physical, and spiritual realms. The themes and cellular memories intersect, sparking a genesis of spirit that fits itself into a body unique unto itself. Of billions of thumbprints, not another like it.

Yet some inexplicable connecting link allows us to feel each other's pain, physical and real. Many of those bodily pains come from pathways that mysteriously jump from one body to another without even physical proximity. This one act defies aloneness and isolation.

To take in someone's pain is like an immune system that has no discretion. Not distinguishing oneself from another does not save the other; it only exhausts the energy and causes the body to disintegrate, as if treading two lives at once. How many children's upset stomachs belong to their parents, how many emotions of parents are borrowed from their children? That this occurs is proof enough of the unbroken thread between us.

Are our dreams in the night the screams of another's life? Past pain, joy, or passion and even thoughtforms invade human isolation.

When I was a child, I often found myself rummaging around in someone else's mind. Sometimes I could not distinguish whether the conversation was going on out loud, or even which of us was speaking.

"I know," I'd say.

"You know what?" they'd ask.

"What you said about that boy."

"But I haven't said it yet; I was just thinking it."

"Oh."......

I didn't understand the ramifications of such activities, then — how they made me a sieve, so permeable to the bodies of others.

Feeling what another feels serves no good purpose to the body which must eventually teach the consciousness to perceive in more subtle realms, to witness from compassion's heart and thus to lift above all sorrows and disease.

In the beginning, when I practiced healing, I would feel physical sensations in my body that belonged to the person I was working on. It helped me to know the source of their trouble. Perhaps it was the only way I could trust myself. Initially, most of us have at least some illusion that we are doing something; that we are connected to the act of healing. Eventually we all must learn to let the flailing ego die.

I know now that it was my urgent karmic plea to help, not only because of my compassion, but because deep in the tracks of my Soul was the obligation to fulfill a debt accrued in some incarnational experience of the body — a debt to caress that which I had once destroyed. This cellular knowing is what attached itself to the evidence of connection brought by pain.

We talk, you and I, even when we think we are hiding. Involuntary leaps of knowing pass from one body to the other. It happens if we want to, or even if we don't. But why does it occur?

Am I in your body? Are you in *mine*?

How can it pass without a channel, without a touch?

It travels past time, through subtle bodies by means of **consciousness** alone.

SOUL BODIES

"The Soul will eternally incarnate. It will renew itself by taking form, just as we renew ourselves by returning to essence!"

I feel as if you are here with me, that I am speaking directly to you. It is as if we have a personal relationship and what I am describing is something I am telling you directly.

I can almost hear your breathing as you are listening to me.

I feel as if I am listening to you too, and that actually it is you that is directing the content of what I am communicating.

It is as if I could hear your comments and questions and perhaps even some of these stories are really yours, because in some way I am listening beyond your mind, into your very Soul.

It is true that we are one Soul family and indeed, within the infinite liquidity of cosmic knowing, all that you experience is a part of me and all that I am is a part of you. How is it that we have forgotten for so long that we live inside each other ? We dream of each other and yet we think we cannot even touch.

Our Soul Bodies are made of the same essence. They have burst into the world of molecules for the same purpose and know each other from beyond matter. Our physical form may appear to be separate and even very different, but the life force that holds the form is made of pure energy which surrounds us both and is everywhere between us. That energy carries our thoughts and feelings so that we are each swirling within the same sea of existence, exposed to the same potentials and pollutants.

You think your doubts and sorrows are yours. They may actually be coming from someone else. Everything we think or feel enters the etheric currents which sweep out from us around the planet and beyond. You are absorbing my thoughts, and I yours. Do not be afraid to be a part of me. If you allow me, I will add great enrichment to your life. Whatever there is about me that you would not want is either already a mirror of you, or could not stick to you unless it were also a part of you. I am not afraid of you. I know that we must teach each other.

We are here to help each other to evolve. None of our choices or experiences could ever damage our magnificent Souls. People are so frightened about what others are thinking, mostly because their own thoughts are so negative.

What if our thoughts become conscious? We would know once and for all that life is what we *think* it to be; because we manifest our own prophecies, we would instantly see the connection between the unmanifest and material worlds. We could place a thought into the void and watch it gather strength as it magnetizes corresponding energies, until it reaches critical mass and explodes into form. How could we then pretend it was not related to us, that we were the victims of something outside us?

Because we view each other from separate bodies, we experience an illusion of distance and isolation that constantly reminds us of our aloneness. This causes us to desperately cling to each other, projecting our relationship to Divine Source onto each other.

The illusion of separation is as old as the experience of translating essence into matter, of incarnating into form. Influenced by outside conclusions, we have lost our direct experience of the worlds outside our third dimension and forgotten tha/ extends beyond body, and even mind.

You and I are a part of something infinitely bigger tha.. physical reality. Though we are not solely our bodies, they seem to cause our forgetfulness and therefore our anguish of separation from Source. In truth, it is not our bodies that separate us from it; it is our bodies that are its expression. Without form, the universe would have no structure upon which to evolve and so would cease to exist.

The Soul will eternally incarnate. It will renew itself by taking form just as we renew ourselves by returning to essence! Infinite variety and environment await the Soul's choice of form, not always to be birthed on Planet Earth or even as a human.

In fact, all humans have inherited a cosmic, genetic encoding that has condensed down from subtle dimensions of light and space. Our physical form actually consists mostly of light, water, and space.

Ultraviolet light is the transmitter of DNA messages which can replicate cells almost infinitely. Every cell holds and nourishes itself through light. Our master glands are extremely light sensitive and the retinic cells of our eyes and pineal glands witness the streams of light fibers that extend from our electromagnetic, auric field.

Water is the maternal sea of cellular existence. Our blood carries the same constituents as the sea and nearly all cellular transactions occur in a liquid medium. Water is life to us. The brain is 90% water and at birth we are juicy little drops of 80% water.

We have difficulty recognizing ourselves as space. Our Emotional Body wants to feel itself safe in the womb of limited reality so that it can avoid its greatest fear of separated isolation.

Can you even imagine yourself as space ? It can be very frightening to your ego to be free of constraint, because its very bondage defines it. The ego becomes anxious when it loses solidity, yet the experience of becoming space guides the ego into the realm of transcendence. You are the impregnated void, swirling in and out of form to gather new energies.

Whenever you become embroiled in any kind of situation that overwhelms you and you cannot see your way out, or you begin to contract into defensiveness, just take a deep breath and begin expanding until you can perceive that the difficulty is but a dot in infinite space. Imagine that you are the whole universe and as you surround the problem, you activate or shift the energy balance. My Higher Self always tells me to transcend adversity by expanding. It truly works !

As a young teenager, I saw a documentary of a great Brazilian psychic surgeon who used old knives to operate, especially on the eyes. Later I had the opportunity to know and experience the work of several Filipino psychic surgeons. When asked how they did it, they described entering the body through the spaces between the cells. For them, the body is made up of infinite space.

I will never forget the shock of my first experience of psychic surgery on my own body. Having read and viewed films demonstrating the process, I was burning with desire to do it myself. Two brothers came to Albuquerque and I went with a friend to see them.

When we arrived, we were all seated and asked to wait in a prayerful state. My entire body became filled with an intense electrical current as I fantasized performing the psychic surgery myself.

As I sat there, a most excruciating tingling began in the tips of all of my fingers. It felt as if there were a million pin pricks causing each finger to become a swollen bulb of light. I knew I was ready and that I would be able to slip through the spaces between the cells, to the points of negative energy that were calling to be released.

Finally, one of the psychic surgeons arrived and began to give a sermon on the evils of man. For almost an hour and a half, he preached in broken English about our limitations and sins. I could see that he was using this as a technique to place himself in an altered state of consciousness and to remove his ego, so that only

God was working through him. Its effect on me, however, was to lose touch with that wonderful feeling of infinite expansion; my ego was gone but so was my inspiration.

When at last it was my turn to enter the room and lie upon the table, I asked the two brothers to allow me to watch the procedure. One put his hand over my eyes and told me to keep them closed. I was attempting to argue the point when I felt the most astounding feeling I have ever felt in my body.

First, I felt the pressure of his hand in my belly. The pressure increased until suddenly there was a kind of inner explosion, accompanied by a loud, internal popping sound. I felt myself go into a state of shock as something was released from inside me. I vaguely realized that he had drawn some kind of small mass out of me. Still more incongruent was a warm trickle of liquid that flowed out of my belly onto my arm at the side of my body.

What held my attention was that this fluid did not cool off as it should if he had poured it on as part of the treatment. No, this was definitely a part of me, a very deep part that was now exposed to the outside world. It was as if I had been split open and my entire inner self were laying there vulnerable to the world.

It was not just my flesh body, but my subtle bodies as well. While my physical and emotional bodies felt the wind of exposure so intensely, my mental and spiritual bodies were experiencing a state of absolute elation. It was the kind of thrilling expansion I have only encountered during my six near-death experiences, when the energy rushed out of my body into the light.

Years later, I had the magnificent opportunity to witness Alex Orbito, the world renowned Filipino psychic surgeon, perform five hundred surgeries at The Light Institute. It was he that explained how, with God's grace, he moves between the spaces of the cells to gather negative energies and remove them from the body.

Space is not the empty void we perceive it to be. It is a creative soup, filled with particles of life waiting for the impetus to translate from essence energy to physical form.

Our bodies are the perfect vehicle to fuse essence and form. Their source material includes all the creations of our earthly evolutionary ladder, as well as cosmic designs from all around our universe. The greatest possible adventure awaits our conscious connection to all the other species within that ladder. We have so much to learn from them about survival, Earth history, and more.

Can you imagine how important it could be for us as a species to learn from the algae (which are the oldest living beings on the planet) how they have survived all the cataclysmic events that have occurred on Mother Earth ? How they use the sunlight to live, and how we could activate our Light Bodies? How the grasshoppers make enzymes that protect them in the presence of radiation ? How sharks hold a secret of health in their cartilage?

The questions are almost infinite. It is so archaic to hold onto the mistaken idea that intelligence only correlates to the size of the brain. We must seek the information held in the mind of the cell and therefore initiate communication with other species through a different path of consciousness.

As we explore the multi-dimensionality of our DNA and that of other species, we will comprehend the thread that links us together, as well as our own unique attributes. Everything existing in body, even a Light Body, has a characteristic "signature."

You have a signature as well, though it would be hard to describe how we recognize you. We might say that it is just a feeling of your presence, or even a subtle body smell. It is more than your physical self, more than the energy that emanates from you. It is something even deeper that makes you familiar to us and we recognize it and know that it is you.

Though science has not found it yet, there can be no doubt that this signature exists within your emotional and spiritual DNA and is re-inherited by you through each of the bodies into which you incarnate. That is why when we meet for the first time we say,

"Oh it's you again. I know you!"

And we proceed to pick up our relationship where we left off, ten years or ten lifetimes ago.

It could be subtle gestures that trigger the recognition. Most assuredly it will have to do with the way your body composes itself.

The body you had in that lifetime will bring some physical characteristic of itself into your present body. Perhaps it is the way your nose sits on your face that reminds me. It may suggest a Greek or Roman lifetime we shared. No one else will notice it, but I will, and I will carry on certain subconscious innuendoes with you that are related to our sojourn together.

Without even looking at your body, you could probably tell me a number of ways you think it is imbalanced in its physical composition, or disconnected by parts which don't seem to fit together.

Your lips, ears, legs, neck, head, and feet are all holding memories of their bodily experiences in other lives. The stories they tell are fantastic and very illuminating! For example, the Romans had very heavy, pole-like legs. They were perfect for marching and conquering. If you have those kinds of legs, think about your yang, forceful energy and how you express it. Those legs could be a great advantage to your present pursuits.

Your physical characteristics may relate to cultural attributes in which whole societies express certain themes through bodily aptitudes. Evolutionists constantly theorize about species adaptations that increase the potential of survival. It is quite possible that individual characteristics are indicators of thematic predilections as much as when they are present in whole groups of people.

Surprisingly, it is just as easy to recognize our emotional DNA from other lifetimes as it is our physical DNA. Mothers often describe how their babies have had specific personalities even before birth. Babies in the womb express emotional aptitudes and seem to react to external vibrations such as music, movies, and the thoughts and feelings of both mother and father from some repertoire of their own.

Mothers describe that response not only in physical terms such as kicking or rolling, but also feel they can detect emotional qualities (which may be transmitted biochemically). After the child is born, that passivity or passion continues to be characteristic of his or her emotional expression.

It is a tremendous gift to discover that the source of many inexplicable emotional behaviors or attitudes are born from other experiences of the Soul, so we need not waste our energy on blame or projection onto parents and others around us.

Tendencies towards uncontrollable anger, jealousies, phobias, and many other distressing behaviorisms can be found to be securely anchored in other lifetimes. At the moment of conception, they piggybacked onto the genetic encoding, in the form of emotional DNA. When we return to their source, they often disappear completely.

Perhaps you suffer bouts of sadness or depression, without being able to put your finger on the cause. It may have been inherited from yourself as the result of an experience that is not a part of your present repertoire, but which haunts your feelings.

I am saying something that I hope will cause you to contemplate very deeply. I am saying that experience penetrates form in such a way as to absolutely affect the future!

Perhaps at some point your mind will shut down in the grip of denial because of what you are shown in this book. It is possible that even the denial is nothing more than a part of you which lies sleeping. We are awakening, you and I, to a depth of remembrance, a quality of knowing that is here to facilitate a restructuring of future potential: our own new bodies. They will hold qualities already known to us and some that we cannot envision as defining humans.

How would you design a new species of humans? If you were creating them, would you place there the unconditional love of the angels, the compassion and guidance of the great Avatars, the devic and galactic mastery of physical laws? Since you can only imagine what already exists, these potential aspects must be even now within your reach!

What is it in the angels that you would wish were in you? Is it their inner peace, their unconditional love? Those qualities are actually embedded in their genetic material. Perhaps it is hard to imagine that they have DNA encoding (since we think of them as ethereal, rather than mortal), but they are a species just as are we.

We are here to provide an anchor for a new species of humans, in which the past/future elements of other species (as well as our own) are recombined. Just imagine a combination of angelics and galactics which could fuse together to correct imbalances in our human form and psyche.

We long to have the power, beauty, and intelligence we project onto others around us. It is almost unfathomable to imagine that we could look out into the universe and hope to attain the attributes we envision held by other, legendary beings.

The brilliant Soul designs exactly the shape and style body we need to bring its essence into form. Every detail of its inheritance is orchestrated to fulfill its purpose. We think we inherit our bodies from our parents, but actually we have collectively contributed to those attributes which become our familial signatures. The Soul who is to play the child might set in motion a bodily weakness within the parent, so that the proper karmic environment is in play for their emotional or spiritual sojourn together. It is the same conversation as when a grandparent reincarnates as their own grandchild: being born to their own child in order to continue a karmic theme they are working on together.

To be born into the third dimension, the unlimited Soul must crystallize itself into a concentration of specific energy. This process of fusion between the egg and the sperm is preceded by a kind of "meltdown," in which the essence material concentrates itself into the receptacle of the body.

Unfortunately, the human genetic encoding carries old, negative conclusions about coming into body that have made it difficult for us to hold the ecstatic intention of the Soul to incarnate. Rather, we tend to fixate our awareness on the pain and fear of the process.

Actually, meltdown occurs at both conception and death. At birth, it is the pure essence that condenses itself into a liquid drop of impregnated matter. At death, it is the combustive meltdown of that matter, back into the ethers.

I have found that about 80% of the people I work with were gripped with fear at the moment of birth and came into life screaming a resounding "NO." This must be erased if we are to inherit our true destiny. Meltdown is merely a process of transitioning in and out of body, and we can learn to do it with grace if consciousness holds its purpose.

In one of my lifetimes, I experienced a singularly terrifying meltdown that needed to be released so that I could learn to embrace embodiment as a great adventure and mission of the Soul. Let me tell it to you now, so that if you, too, have deeply engraved fears of coming into body, you can dissolve them as well.

MELTDOWN

*It is so sorrowful to let the lights go down from this enlight-
ened mind — to not remember and thus solidify into body and,
surrendering the brightness of true life, to slumber in the form
of matter whilst all of heaven sings ... and hear it not.*

I became aware of the screams as if I were coming out of a
long, heavy nightmare. Little by little I heard their intensity and
pitch, but from a frozen, leaden place. I could not know what to do
or how to do it.

The screams emanated from very far away at first, but as I
listened, it seemed as if I were traveling along the thread of sound
until I connected to something unfathomable and yet somehow of
myself. In an instant of combustion, we burst into a searing fire-
ball, then nothingness.

Once again the sound intensified until it almost consumed my
consciousness. Blinking in and out of awareness, I awakened
abruptly in the middle of a scream and was gripped by the petrify-
ing realization that the horrifying sounds were coming from me. I
struggled to discover how I was making the screams.

It was a vibrating mechanism which I located a small distance
from my point of awareness. In a flash, I was inside the sound box
and felt the screeching shock waves pass through me and out in
every direction. I was the scream.

Now the direction of energy shifted, and I found the cause of the scream. My consciousness was being fused down through the eye of a diamond into a body of mortal scope — a human form. It was the impact of that point at the eye of the diamond that invented the scream.

Pain, terrible pain, coursed through my consciousness. It was a dynamic light vehicle being thrust into a resisting wall of dense matter. One was the pulse of life itself, the other carved out of the darkness of denial.

The pain belonged to both bodies. The crucible of fire forged a point of intersection in which the light was molded into a dense body, through a searing slow burn into carnate form. The meltdown of my Light Body was the cause of the excruciating sensations and forced the reaction of crying out. Again and again the experience was repeated in a torturously slow-motion pattern, as if it were essential that I record in my consciousness just how embodiment occurs — not from the lofty pronouncement of the Soul, but from the actuality of the material world.

I know the point is not to conclude that embodiment is punishment by pain, but rather to witness the energetic equations of the manifest and the unmanifest. Since pain comes from resisting matter, on levels of higher consciousness it relates to spiritual acuity rather than sensory, experiential channels. I was definitely resisting the slowing-down process and paying the consequences.

It is certainly not true that every incarnation is initiated by pain. In fact, many meltdowns are accompanied by the fluidity of conscious purpose not lost in the translation: to bring heaven on Earth, teach unconditional love, manifest divine laws, and infinite other sacred intentions.

That particular body belonged to the "Time of Christ" period of 2,000 years ago, when the human form had become encrusted in a kind of slowness that bore a great degree of physical and psychic density. The purpose of the mission was to instill a new lightness within the genetic material of humankind. The evolutionary alchemy has been activated at various strategic points, when the existing genetic makeup of the species has not adapted well enough to ensure survival, or any beneficial advancement.

The alchemy is carried out not by willful interference, but rather through the subtle channels of genetic strands which are seeded and must simply await a point of critical mass in which enough crucial elements are present to activate them directly. At that point, they will become evident and visible in someone, or in a few members of the species, who will then serve to model the variant in such a way that others will consciously select it for themselves. This could take moments or thousands of years, Earth time.

You may not have thought of this before, but I know that you have experienced it directly. Think about how you heard of an idea or even something that happened to someone and suddenly you knew exactly what it was because it had happened to you, yet until that moment you had not been able to put it into a context to understand what it meant. Then suddenly, it all became clear and you knew it as if it had always been true. Your conscious awareness of it makes it a part of your own repertoire.

Actually, we seed each other all the time. Sometimes we lead others into a game of chess in which we have counted all the moves and can predict the outcome. This borders on manipulation, which is outside of Cosmic Law, but we do it because we think we have the right to choose what is best — for ourselves, yes; for others, we do not!

Those other beings who seed us have the very same dilemmas and some of them have served to liberate us, while others have brought only pollutive confusion to the human race.

These seeding missions are done through group Souls which lock together to accomplish the task. So it was with us back then, and each of us had a specialized role that fit into one cohesive plan.

My role was to come into direct contact with the human genetic material and open it up for the seeding. I did this by borrowing the sexual behavior patterns of those people to access the source matrix. I engaged in multiple sexual acts in order to completely scrutinize the patterns of the genetic helix.

Though my body looked like that of a human female, it did not have the same biochemical apparatus — a fact that both facilitated my work and simultaneously got me into trouble.

The characteristic odor of those earthly bodies was something I had to struggle to accommodate. It was very strong and not terribly different from the animals they tended, though more repugnant because of the mixture. In contrast, my body carried an elusive air of perfumed dew. It was an alluring attractant to the males and even the females, causing them to behave in a kind of violent frenzy.

I began my earthly sojourn as a young girl who was fond of sitting on a certain man's lap. There, coiled like a snake in slumber, I was able to lift all of his sexual preferences and experiences directly from his body through a kind of scanning technique. On some level of his being, he knew what I was doing and so he even facilitated my access into the mind of his cells.

He would sit very still until a certain current began to pulse wildly through him and then would abruptly leap up and rush off to find his wife. I would sometimes observe his passion from an unobtrusive opening into his room.

It was through the sexual act that I could view the actual chromosomes and genes. Even as I tell you this story, I can still perceive them as if they are perpetually floating in front of me.

The instant a man inserted his member into my body, the trance state that held us both would take over. I would be absorbed into a field of various-shaped genetic structures. There were L-shaped, half-moon, skewered spirals and other shapes, in several shades of muted colors such as green, brown, and even orange.

From them, I learned biochemical relationships to temperament, physical amenities, familial histories, field dynamics, and other kinds of information I cannot describe to you because human scientists haven't quite discovered them as of yet. Recently, I have had the spectacular revelation that these genetic structures are replicas of the star constellations in our heavens. Perhaps they will provide clues as to our cosmic origin.

Each sexual encounter provided a rich tapestry of information that showed us what needed to be activated or innovated to evolve the species. Unfortunately, whatever had been instilled through their own experience or by "accident" could not be removed from the outside. This fact has led to tremendous disruptions in their genetic evolution.

The law of non-intervention has allowed entire epochs to be marred by de-evolutionary qualities that must be worked out and de-activated by the species' own volition.

We are witnessing some of those destructive genetic aptitudes today, as we watch various groups trying to destroy each other because of thoughtforms belonging to their ancestors (having arisen to active status through a repetitious pattern) being carried out in a world in which they no longer serve a purpose.

Though it was my mission to use my body as a human laboratory, I had not taken into account the degree to which I would instill the realities of the humans of this era into my own consciousness.

The Emotional Body of the humans, rarely present in other species, has a force so powerful and insidious that it infused itself into the matrix of my own vehicle. Levels of anger, envy, and separation became so intertwined with my physical beingness that it has taken these thousands of years to erase them.

Many of those negative expressions came about through the frustrations of conscious entrapment, which all humans suffer because the veil of forgetfulness eclipses the infinite universal oneness. The illusion of separation causes profound fear, which they conceal with their anger.

That nagging inner voice of the brittle ego is characteristic of humans. Tragically, the conversation is always about the lack, the negative, and the unforeseen danger. Constantly whispering innuendoes, it keeps the mind attentive to the blaming, excusing voices and threats to power, which it uses to justify self-righteousness and anger.

I must admit to a good deal of anger myself, stemming from the experience of bodily limitation. While several of my galactic teammates had retained elements of their Light Bodies and could still perform what humans referred to in great awe as "miracles," I was very earthbound, in a body that necessitated sexual penetration in order to experience connectedness!

One of my teammates had the mission of awakening the Earthling's awareness of cosmic law through the demonstration of the Light Body. To do this, he himself had to be schooled in the laws of Earth physics. He was brought before the great masters of the earthly plane, to be taught the kinds of transmutations that were characteristic of human form and which capacities would be useful to model. He was taught to focus and activate both the astral and Light bodies.

Though his energetic essence was capable of the transfiguration of cosmic force, he needed to be instructed in earthly context. Thus he learned the art of manifestation and bilocation, alteration of matter, and atomic healing as they pertained to human intent.

Throughout his travels, he kept his Light Body activated and often affected the outside world from the lofty location of his meditation cave.

When he left his body through the ascension of light, I became disconsolately dejected and enraged at the same time. As I sensed his departure, a most desolate, empty feeling fell upon my body. It was followed by a fury so profound that, through my sheer will, I cast aside the gigantic stone hiding his body. There lay the naked truth of his liberation and my bondage.

Only once in this lifetime have I felt that same energy moving in me: it was a time when an attacker was reaching for me. Without any conscious volition of my own, a thrust of laser-like force came from my solar plexus and threw him to the ground. I had not physically touched him and that realization terrified us both. It is interesting that each of these kinetic acts stemmed from an eruption of anger. I long to practice this power from a place of consciousness. The art of moving matter has been known to humans for eons, and one day we will find its mastery.

In that lifetime, I could not translate the power into just any act of my will. Even though I desperately wanted to be freed from my body, I could not transcend the physical plane in the same way as my companion had done.

I had not been born of a woman, nor had I given birth, and was therefore unable to simply age and die. I had passed through the meltdown and first appeared as a young girl of about eight years of age. Because the purpose of the incarnation had been to record the genetic material through the sexual currents of these people, my own sexual energy was very concentrated, even from the moment I passed through the meltdown. Now, as I suffered to pull up and out of that body, I felt as if I were impregnated with the weight of all human genes. It was a kind of listless inertia that I simply could not surmount.

The shock of being left behind put me into a kind of catatonic state, from which I could not perceive the continuing support of my colleagues. Our team was intertwined through a web of light energy transmission, but I could not sustain myself in this inhospitable environment without the force of that connection.

My dejected Earth body, hunched over on the side of a hill, wrapped in a robin's egg-blue shawl, is a very vivid memory even now. That particular color has always elicited a deeply emotional response from me. My heart always skips a beat when I see it and I feel a deep desire to completely absorb it into my body. What a great healing it has been to find the source of such intense emotion!

To cope with my despondency on the physical plane, I engaged in an intense messaging to my partner who had ascended into the higher realms. I could not eat, would not move, but held my gaze upward, relentlessly calling him to perform the translation of energy I needed to return to full consciousness. Ultimately, he released me from that body and lifted me up and out of its environs.

The meltdown **out** of the body was a much more gentle experience than that of coming into body. It was like a great cosmic sigh. As the Earth body fell away and I was again free to float in the sea of consciousness, I felt the profound relief of being freed from the burdens of that dense reality. I was flooded with the infinite love and oneness that greets us all as we translate into Source.

All my life I have re-experienced that flood of joy when I look upward into the sky. A rush of indescribable ecstasy blasts me through a kind of light barrier and translates my consciousness out of body. Today, I sleep with a glass ceiling over me, and I often get that same exhilarated feeling when I look up into the Milky Way.

OUR BODIES

We Earthlings are so bent on the myth of separation that it is hard to communicate the truth of our oneness. Neither our "self" or even our physical body is one separate entity. It is an illusion to think that, when we pass through the meltdown into form, we are coming into one third-dimensional body. Rather, we are coming into a streaming, loosely woven matrix of particle bodies that inform and support each other.

The mental, physical, emotional, and spiritual bodies are the main facets of this conglomerate Soul echo. Each and all of them bring experiences and themes related to other bodies from other lifetimes, which are still crystallized within the Soul's evolutionary pattern. From the Soul echo within these four main bodies comes the creation of other bodies, such as the Primordial Body, the Light Body, and the Shakti Body.

The Primordial Body is very much the body I was utilizing during that time two thousand years ago. It is the body of survival. The Primordial Body employs the powerful force of instinct to protect itself and find its way. The instinctual sense is a very basic defense mechanism, mostly focused on the preservation of self. It senses danger and also potential opportunities related to procreation.

The Primordial Body is the sexual body that processes all information in terms of reproduction of the species: how to seduce the sperm into direct contact with the egg. Its purpose is to ensure all aspects of mating so that the generations continue.

You can see how it is that we instinctively know when someone is feeling us out as a potential sexual partner, even without any overt gestures. Through these primordial, sexual currents, we can also tell when relationships are out of sync.

The Light Body is the form of the Spiritual Body, the divine spark of the Soul itself. It is the essence and source of all radiance. It brings the whisper of all wisdom and the grace of cosmic motion.

The Shakti Body is born of the reunion of sexual energies with the Light Body. When the sexual currents are released upward from the primordial levels, they become the spark of life force that fuels the cosmic fires. It is another kind of meltdown in which the body melts from its isolated form — its male or female posture — and becomes a life force capable of Divine Fusion. The Shakti Body is the elevated electric pulse that offers kundalini enlightenment, cosmic orgasm, and the bliss of all oneness.

When the Shakti Body is awakened, we can find the quality of perception necessary to center the Soul and simultaneously caress the fringes of our hologram. That vibration sets us free from the sleeping states of karma so that we can find our purpose. Every Soul Body has this potential, although it may lie dormant through many lives.

By combining the Primordial and Light Bodies, you enact the coalescence of the Shakti Body. There is nothing more fascinating than the direct feedback of your own bodies. You can gain astounding self-awareness by practicing the meditation of communing with these bodies. By asking each body to take form, you will enter into the magical reality of creative expression in which their essence qualities are transmitted to you through any of your seventy senses of perception.

Try this meditation for yourself. I recommend that you read it over first or even record it so you will know what to do.

Find a quiet place and begin to breathe into your body. (Don't lie down, as you may fall asleep.)

Place your hand over your genitals to help you focus, and ask your Primordial Body to take form.

Breathe deeply and relax.

Accept the first form that pops into your consciousness. (You may see or hear or feel the presence of your Primordial Body.) It may present itself as a symbol, an object, or as a color.

Allow yourself to perceive the quality of its energy.

Is it angry, lustful, or neglected? Satiated, joyful, or ecstatic?

Ask your Primordial Body what color it needs from you to come into complete balance in your life now.

Draw that color in from the cosmos, into the top of your head, and bring it out through your stomach (solar plexus). Extend it like a ray of light to your Primordial Body.

Continue to send color to it until it changes form or feels as if it is full.

Place your Primordial Body to one side of your vision and proceed to activate your Light Body.

Place the third finger of your right hand very lightly over your third eye (middle of your forehead).

Breathe deeply, in and out, several times.

You will feel a pressure or pulse as the area becomes activated.

Ask your Light Body to take form for you.

The Light Body form is very often more subtle and amorphous, yet its presence is very palpable.

Ask your Light Body what color or colors it needs from you to come into perfect balance in your life now.

Breathe that color into the top of your head and out through your solar plexus to your Light Body and see what happens. When it feels like you have given enough color, place your Light Body to the other side of your vision.

Take a big breath and ask the two bodies to merge together.

You will most likely feel a surge of energy as they meet and create a new energy through their fusion.

Bathe yourself in that wonderful juice which is the life force energy of the Shakti Body.

A Soul melts its essence into the mold of form: a body. The body creates a formula for its lesson, its intention, and purpose. The external structure reflects that purpose through the size and shape, health and balance of all organs and all parts.

This is why each body part carries within it a whole history, a predilection for a particular expression or a magnetic pattern which attracts situations and people (through its electromagnetic field or its biochemical radiance) that correspond with the indelible memory component of the cell (the memory pattern is not destroyed even if the cells themselves disintegrate).

At the end of a life, the body melts its form (to be stored in the structures of the Akashic Records) and its essence escapes into the cosmos. Though the cellular format dissolves in the death process, the emotional and spiritual DNA are retrieved and recorded in the Akashic Records so that these are meted out and included within any other structure or body designed by the Soul. What is held in the Akashic Record becomes the crucible by which the Soul is challenged to thread its way through the karmic mandates, to its own initiation.

THE BODY SPEAKS

We had come to the end now, only one or two questions remained.

"Where are you holding that memory of connection in your body?"

Great sobs of deep-throated tears erupted to fill the spaces of the room. Then, a most poignant silence.

"Everywhere," he said, in the softest of whisperings. "My whole body is filled with it. I feel my heart trembling. It's in my eyes and way down in the pit of my stomach. My skin is being caressed in a pink glow."

Again, the tears falling unabashedly on the sheet.

My own heart held the space as I watched him emerge from his old self, like a shimmering mirage.

It wouldn't matter now how difficult things were; he had set himself free by experiencing this powerful connection to his own Divine Source. After that indelible moment, he heaved a great sigh and lay still on the table for a long while.

As I swept off his field, I looked into his newly opened eyes and thought, "How pure and beautiful are the eyes of the Soul!"

"Where are you holding that first memory of love?"

"Here on my lips," she whispered. "I feel them quivering. It's as if they were electrified by a thousand pin pricks. I am suckling my mother's breasts. I can smell the milk, so warm and sweet. Love is all around me, tender and strong.

"I feel a touch on my head. ... It's my father's hand. He's sending me lights, pink lights. He loves me, too."

Tears ... companions of the healing force.

"Where are you holding the memory of this beautiful death in which you laid your body down and rose up into the heavens?"

"It's in the top of my head. It feels like a gentle breeze. My head is open. It feels so fresh and clear.

"I want to cry. It's so easy ... so ecstatic! I'm soaring upward. I see my body lying there. It looks so peaceful. It's beautiful!

"The light, the light, it's flooding all around me and through me! I am bursting, a trillion sparks of me in every direction. I am the universe!"

Let the body speak and it will show you realms of pure ecstasy and light and even thought, at its very source. The mind of the cell is the passageway between matter and the unmanifest. It holds the blueprint of your Soul's intention into form. Ask where you come from and your body will spin you out into the cosmos and in to your absolute essence.

An experience of such bliss can become the force that transforms your reality. Perhaps it necessitates a new kind of consciousness to realize that such wonderful energy is inside you and not dependent or sourced in something or someone outside you! You do have these kinds of memories in the mind of your cells, and if you ask your body, it will help you to find them.

Each person on the planet at this time has had incarnations of enlightenment in which these ecstatic levels have been attained. Even our present lifetime is full of moments of great joy. It is hard to believe that we would not remember them. The higher emotions feel so fleeting and are difficult to hold in our consciousness because of their fast vibration, in contrast to the lower emotions which are slow and heavy. The intensity of negative states over-shadow the higher ones, although they still exist in encapsulated form, awaiting our awareness.

You can learn to access and use higher emotions to set the frequency of your body. This is very important because your frequency is the beacon that calls all experience to you. The higher frequencies are a part of the fabric of your body. Imagine the ecstasy at the moment of your conception. It still exists within the trillion of cells that emerged from that first impregnated ovum!

There is nothing your body does not know, does not remember on some level of its being, from the moment of conception onward or into infinite lifetime experiences. Like a dream computer of limitless bytes, the body mind can never become too full to record. It holds all experience and all relativity. It can separate out memories, desires, and intersecting links of association in an end-less swirling mass of life force energy. These memories are like echoes that continue to ripple out from the core of your being to influence all of your life.

BODY ECHOES

Your body utilizes the echoes of its experiences to perceive its destiny and describe itself in terms of the energies moving within it. It's a kind of body echo that amplifies the memories stored within the mind of the cell and brings them to the surface of bodily and emotional expression. It literally builds itself on the echoes by attracting situations which verify these self-identifications and by creating ever new possibilities of repetition.

A most influential echo is that of the prophecies of others. A parent, a teacher, a friend might make a comment about who you are and it sticks with you forever. Even if you forget the episode, its echo will resound within the infrastructure of your being.

I remember when I was 21 years old and an eye doctor informed me that by the time I was 40, I would be so blind, I wouldn't be able to read. It threw me into a deep sense of depression because reading was a part of my everyday pattern. After several days of sorrow, my Higher Self gave me a message that I did not understand at all. It said, "You are the book!"

Indeed, I found that reading gave me headaches, and I ultimately gave up reading all but technical material. I wandered about more frequently outside where my farsightedness expanded my field of perception. I began to "daydream" more, visions came and magnificent cosmic conversations began to play upon my consciousness.

However, the prediction stuck and I found myself with rather poor eyesight in terms of anything written. Perhaps some of the blurring is a kind of occupational hazard related to looking at energy fields, but this too, is just a fulfilling of the prophecy. Recently, I met a man who told me that his eyesight had been 20/200 until one day he realized that this poor vision was just a thought form and since our cells are completely exchanged within seven year cycles, he could have clear and healthy eyesight if he chose to focus on his fresh, new cells. He began to signal this to his ocular cells and now he prides himself in his 20/40 vision! What a perfect example of how consciousness can affect our body echoes, which are composed of old thoughtforms, prophecies, and predictions.

Stop for a moment and ask yourself what prophecies you have internalized, and what predictions you have held inside that others placed on you? Are there echoes such as "You'll never make it," "You're dumb," and "You can't see past your nose!"?

It is true that we humans seem to thrive on negativity as a stimulus to growth, but it needn't be that way. We could learn through our great joy and pleasure, just as well. All experience ultimately reflects the Soul's design, and body echoes can represent communications of great spiritual depth.

As energetic imprints, body echoes are not limited to your present body, but are also the echoes of **all** the bodies you have created. They hold great love, wisdom, courage, and clarity. Through your body's conscious pathways, you can retrieve these more positive echoes and utilize their effect on your life now.

When your consciousness touches the point of memory that stores these kinds of sensations, there is a change in the body itself. It vibrates, giggles, sighs; it becomes happy and whole. Can you imagine how magnificent it is to experience such feelings in your body? It is so willing to show you a range of expression you may have long forgotten, or never even knew existed.

The book of life is a fascinating one. Why not pluck a memory right now for yourself and see what comes into your consciousness?

Let us use the question of love since it is so important a theme for our sojourn on Earth.

Take a deep breath, as if you could fill up your whole body with just one inhalation.

Ask your body to show you the part of your body that is holding a memory of love.

Relax completely and be receptive to any signals you get from your body.

Repeat the question, "Where am I holding a memory of love?"

You may feel a little sensation in some part of your body.

You may hear a word in your mind, throat, stomach, hands, or elsewhere.

You may see a part of your body.

Whatever impression you receive, simply bring your conscious awareness to that part of your body.

Imagine that you are breathing in and out through that place, and in a moment you will experience the memory coming to light.

You may be surprised about what is revealed. It could be a memory of receiving love or giving love. It may be a platonic love, rather than a romantic one. It might be a love shared with a tree, an animal, a flower.

Allow yourself to taste the memory fully: all its smells, sounds, touches, and feelings.

When you feel complete with the energy of that love, command all the trillions of cells in your body to imprint that love (not the memory itself), so that it is everywhere in your body.

Some echoes are recordings of teachings you have selected to balance karma and may even be painful to your conscious psyche (which would not at present make the same choices, having seen their folly). Their presence calls forth repetitive patterns in which you seem to find yourself in the same kind of situations or relationships again and again, without understanding why.

You always have the freedom to learn lessons in any way you choose, but the emotional energies of passion and guilt stored from past incarnations often override the more enlightened choice, and provoke a re-enactment within the same energetic strata as before. Sometimes it seems as if we repeat and repeat the very things we are trying to avoid.

It is the old "eye for an eye" style of reparation, only this time it is probable that you will be the one who suffers the consequences, and you who deals out the punishment. As the emotional associations and conclusions lurk within the mind of the cell, they create destructive energies that magnetize negativity. Thankfully, they can be cleared by finding where they are stored in the body and erasing them. You can literally wash them away through the power of consciousness and the force of Light.

BODYSCAPES

The body echoes are a part of a deeper patterning called the bodyscape. It is an infinite tapestry of senses and perceptual fields, creating a holographic scenario for the energy of the Soul. The body speaks within the form — the living pulse of all experience — and the Soul is there. The bodyscape spans the horizon and brings into focus the specific scenarios of the lessons that shape our memories. These are strung together by our Emotional Body, which correlates emotional intensity with physical bodies, places, and visual scenes that tell the life story of each body. Bodyscapes connect us to the physical world. They are the source of the déjà vu that you might experience when coming into a new landscape and yet feeling as if you had been there before.

Indeed, the bodyscape is like a landscape, but it is your body in its own scenario. A body echo would be the "energy" of a feeling, for example, which would be held in some part of the body, but the bodyscape would be the actual *experience* of that energy, the *source* of that feeling. You could view the people and the place of the scene, the smells and other perceptual associations, just as you actually experienced them. You would view the bodyscape as if it were frozen on a screen. The entire episode will be encapsulated and if you say, "take me back to my first experience of that feeling in this life," you will see the whole scene just as it occurred. That first experience triggered the reticular activating system of the brain and was recorded so that any subsequent experiences would be referenced there and associated with it by the Emotional Body. It is still crystallized and can be plucked out of the body intact. When you can break open and dissolve a bodyscape through the power of consciousness, it completely changes who you are and how the body perceives reality.

PHOBIAS

This is the case with phobias, in which a fear seems to have no direct causative event at its source and yet it is expressed with such intense reaction that the body is left paralyzed in its grip. The phobic echo does have a source, however, even if it has been "inherited" from someone else or its energetic memory comes from beyond the present body. The person usually has no recollection of the source of the fear, just an awareness of its paralyzing effect on the body. Fascinatingly, when the corresponding bodyscape is uncovered and released, so too is the phobia itself! Here is an example of its workings on the psyche given me by one of my students who is an artist:

Phobia: An unusual fear of chicken feathers with an accompanying dislike and fear of traditional African art, abhorring the colors of yellow, red, brown, and black.

"In my early childhood I experienced a terror of anything related to chickens. I could not sleep with comforters or pillows made of feathers and I found them dirty. I also had nightmares in which dark faces chased me and I woke up crying every night for almost two years. Though I was allowed to sleep with my parents when I was sick, I was terrified of the African statues in their room and felt that they actually made me sick.

"*As I grew older, I despised African art, though I was interested in African people and thought them more beautiful than myself, who was so 'bland' looking.*"

Session to reveal the source of her phobia:

"*I see colors of mainly orange, red, yellow, brown, and black. ... I see an African man standing in front of an altar. The scene is in the same colors that I first saw. There is a woman on the altar. Her body is covered with chicken feathers and blood. I am the black man. I am a Voodoo priest. The woman died during the ritual. I cut her throat. ... There are many ugly looking statues made out of black wood.*

"*There are many people trapped in caves. They died at my command. An older priest kills the chickens and collects the blood and feathers for the ritual. He needs to have specific skills. The ritual demands certain steps.*

"*I feel no other feelings than the sense of power. I see this life-force energy in women. I want to get it*

"*At the end of the session I release all the people I killed in that lifetime into the light. I also release the entrapped spirit of the African priest.*"

Results:

"*I lost the feeling that feathers are dirty. I started to understand why feathers are sacred in other traditions. I felt a powerful release from guilt and self-judgment. Immediately after the session, I began feeling a higher energy in my body at night. I discovered that I can heal with my hands.*"

FLASHBACKS

Flashbacks are another interesting form of bodyscape. Unpredictably, out of nowhere, the scene of some dramatic event will suddenly overtake the visual or auditory channels and crowd out all other stimuli. They can occur when a person is experiencing stress or anxiety because these states excite the Emotional Body to overlap its channels of association. Sometimes they happen like a nightmare while sleeping and even during normal waking states. Time doesn't seem to be a factor, as they re-occur long after the initial experience. This is a terrible reality that many war veterans suffer; they cannot be healed with drugs, but rather by actually releasing the bodyscape energetically.

Drug-induced flashbacks are also very debilitating and disorientating because they surface as a scene that may not relate to physical reality, but might be an emotionally charged field of colors or patterns. Flashbacks can bring a person right to the edge of insanity, and they definitely pollute the psychic airways.

The bodyscape is composed of all the life vignettes that encompass our Soul themes. Through its window, we can look upon encapsulated memories of such epic explorations as love, power, sexuality, spirituality, and life purpose. Bodyscapes exist within the mind of the cell and are drawn on the fabric of all our organs and body parts, which hold them intact even though we change body "dwellings." They are not erased when the body dies. They are locked within the spiritual DNA that becomes the resource material for future scenarios and bodies.

At The Light Institute, we view the bodyscapes through the window of multi-incarnations. For each incarnation, the Soul selects a body that will allow it to practice its evolutionary choices. The incarnational memories stored in the body are so powerful that they literally shape our destiny because of their magnetic quality to attract certain kinds of energy. Upon the form of that body are laid the scenes of all the experiences that will ultimately influence the energetic composition of yet another body.

The trick is to have consciousness of what we are learning through these experiences and themes. Otherwise we just keep doing it and it takes a million bodyscapes to fill up a capsule, so we aren't going anywhere very fast. The moment we apply conscious-ness and ask, "What was the Soul learning, and in what lifetime?" and we focus in on it, we can take what would have been many lifetimes, encapsulate them into one lifetime and unfold the whole universe from the point of "now." It becomes the force that ripples out through all the other lifetimes and dissolves the spin points or connecting links between incarnational themes. The spin point is the threshold of the evolutionary spiral. It is holding all the threads of the associations between lifetimes, so that if you pluck that one, you do not have to go through all the rest. They can't connect any-more; the fabric is torn and that is what speeds karma and quickens the evolution of a particular theme.

The bodyscapes become spectacular tools in terms of under-standing what is happening in your life now. If you contemplate the major themes you are witnessing and then allow the body to show you the bodyscapes that relate to them, you will have a very holographic view of how the law of karma is being played out.

Through theme sessions at The Light Institute, you can dis-cover the source of any pattern that persists into today. We often do specific workshops designed to uncover the "point of source" of a theme, then clear and dissolve it completely from the body.

The bodyscapes will yield the memories stored in the body, to be released or amplified as mind- or body-altering energies that bring amazing changes to the experience of reality. These breath-less encounters with the body's deepest energies are absolutely real and the person having them feels a profound awakening in terms of being in body. Sometimes when people awaken to their incarnational memories, their whole body structure changes for no other reason than they are activating that imprinting within the genetic material, and the body reshapes itself. There are literally thousands of bodyscapes within you, each one reflecting a facet of your true potential and signature. Instead of being cut off from all that is magical, you can experience it inside you.

As you initiate these fantastic conversations with your body and experience how eloquently it speaks, you will know that it holds the secrets of your Soul. *The body expresses the Soul through structure and form.* It is a living road map that gives the clues as to what is held within its parts and organs and cells. Though each body is unique, there is a universal blueprint that designates basic patterns of purpose, related to the functionality of the cellular groupings and body parts. This blueprint itself becomes a kind of body language that speaks of physical, emotional, mental, and spiritual energies. To study the blueprint is to listen, at the most profound level, to what the body speaks!

Because the body is holographic and multi-dimensional, when we focus on any particular area, we must remember that we are looking at just one level, which is connected to other levels or facets through the streaming channels of energy. Though we may see it on a vertical plane in which the bottom and the top seem separated, they are actually touching through an interconnecting web of consciousness.

The focus of the body follows the more subtle channels of the energetic centers (or *chakras*) in terms of communicative stratification.

Thus, the first chakra in the pelvic area is the "touch me" expression of the Primordial Body.

The solar plexus chakra in the stomach area calls out, "help me," and holds the themes of the Emotional Body.

The heart chakra whispers, "feel me," and invites relationship.

The throat chakra says, "tell me," and begs communication with you from the depth of your truth.

The third-eye chakra flashes "see me" into your psyche, and hints the wisdom of clairvoyance.

The crown chakra opens the thousand-petaled lotus and celebrates the mastery of knowing. "Know me," it calls out to the whole universe.

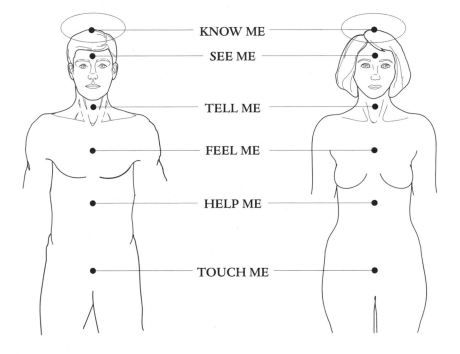

KNOW ME

SEE ME

TELL ME

FEEL ME

HELP ME

TOUCH ME

CHAKRIC THEMES

BODY PARTS

The body wears the mask of the Soul and paints itself in the colors of infinite lifetimes. It stretches and molds its parts to echo the bodies of a thousand mothers' mothers, and fathers' fathers. It speaks in symbols and shapes to convey its longing, its memory, its source.

Each cell holds the whole, the story of its sojourn, the potential of its purpose. The mind of the cell is the concert of scribes, diligently recording all thought, all sight and sound, all perception. The atoms weave their dance of infinity, passing back and forth through the window of form to the formless. Every cell re-enacts creation as it becomes, itself, the designer of its own future. Perhaps that is why we linger in the past, so intimate and close, not listening to the approaching winds that bring (ourselves) again.

Each organ and part of the body participates in the overall design. It is the art of the Soul. The heart, the eyes, the hands, and head each speak the language of truth; the body never lies. All that occurs to the body does so in conversation with the Soul, which allows all, loves all, knows all.

The Soul uses the body as its instrument of growth. Each illness or accident to any part tells us what our body needs to find its equilibrium and point of growth. The body whispers, then speaks, and ultimately shouts its truth, until we somehow begin to pay attention to its message.

Though each of us has our own unique experiences and memories held within any part or organ of the body, the body itself will file those experiences in some corresponding relationship with the symbolic code of its parts. It is fascinating to comprehend that the symbolic and the functional aspects coincide.

Let us look at that code, the better to commune with our bodies:

THE HEAD:

The center of thought. The control part of the body. Associated with mental reality; the computer. Many people have isolated themselves in the head and do not experience their bodies or emotions directly. They only feel safe by *thinking about life*.

BACK OF THE HEAD:

The occipital ridge corresponds to toxins stored from the blood.

TOP OF THE HEAD:

The release of bodily energies through the crown chakra. Connection to higher energies. Conversely, headaches in this area are often an expression of negative feelings about being in body, as in the theme of allergies which conveys feelings of *being overwhelmed by life*. Allergies trigger the sense of vulnerability by which something in the outside world overpowers the body.

GROOVE WHERE HEAD ATTACHES TO NECK:

The opening where light enters the head. Holds "Window to the Sky" points of higher consciousness.

FACE:

Where we show who we are or hide behind a mask of culturally prescribed defenses. (See facial shapes on pages 65–68 for symbolic reference.)

EYES:

Themes of what we want to see or not see. Windows to the Soul: the left eye is the inner, spiritual vision and the right eye relates to the outer world of the ego. The eyes are the organs of the liver in Chinese medicine and therefore are connected to purification, levels of energy, and anger.

TEMPLES:

Relate to the *wei chi* energy, which is the energy that protects us from "evil chi" (invading energies such as viruses and negative force fields). The temples correspond to the gall bladder meridian and the "official" in charge of decision-making.

NOSE:

The organ of the heart. Large and bulbous noses correspond to both the physical and emotional functions of the heart. Psychics often have large noses. Breathing issues relate to unconscious feelings about being in body. The sense of smell gives pleasure to embodiment.

CHEEKS:

Store emotions. Round faces intensify emotional potential and signal that emotional themes are important lessons for this body.

EARS:

The external ear holds acupuncture points that reflex directly to every part and organ of the body. The ears are the organs of the kidneys and therefore relate to themes of fear and to our willingness to listen both to ourselves and the outside world. The inner ear is crucial to our sense of balance; physically, emotionally, and spiritually.

TMJ:

Where the upper and lower jaws meet. People often have imbalanced TMJ joints that pop out and cause pain. Point of intersection for energies into the head. Where we store anger, resentment, and a sense of impotence.

LIPS:

Reflex to the intestines. When there is toxic and irritating blockage in intestines, people often get herpes blisters on their lips. This is why taking acidophilus and other flora that re-balance the intestines will often stop the blisters. The lips are the first point of intimate contact and express feelings of affection. Lips express sexuality. Full lips indicate very sensual people. Tight or thin lips speak of a holding back.

CHIN:

Expresses defensive strength. Underdeveloped chins, especially in men, indicate a more passive personality, not wishing to take control. The chin holds acupuncture points related to the sexual glands.

THROAT:

Center of communication where we give voice to thoughts and feelings. The throat chakra is a union point of yin/yang energy balance. We also hold self-righteousness and judgment in the throat. As a Soul group, we are all working on the throat chakra level. We must learn how to communicate our knowing and our truth. If the heart is open and the higher centers of consciousness are activated, the quality of expression can be most exquisite. The throat holds the thyroid gland, which influences all the energy levels of the body.

NECK:

Where we hold our will. When we are rigid and willful in our perspective, we often have "stiff" necks or other difficulties of the neck. The seventh cervical vertebra, which forms the large bump at the base of the neck, is where the yang meridians come together. It is a common place of psychic leakage when we lack focus.

SHOULDERS:

Represent the sense of burden or responsibility. Sloping or "drooping" shoulders are a yin expression of defeat. Rolled-forward shoulders speak of lack of confidence. Pressed-back shoulders may be a yang, defiant stance. The left shoulder represents family karma. The right shoulder represents external responsibility in terms of the world, visibility, manifestation.

ARMS:

The giving and receiving of love. The left arm is the yin *receiver* of energies. The right arm is the yang *expresser*, which manifests and gives energy. Though balanced healers can use their arms equally, they usually take energy with the left hand and give it with the right.

WRISTS:

Flexibility. Important chakras controlling energies coming into the body. Crucial for healers who do "laying on of hands" or who sweep the body field and flick the residues off through the wrists.

HANDS:

Force of creativity. Emotional expression, power of touch. Carpal tunnel disease is on the rise not only because of specific occupational activities such as computer use, but it emotionally corresponds to inner conflicts, dejection, and a feeling of "I can't do it."

FINGERS:

The fingers are primary entry and exit points of energy. Each finger tip holds acupuncture points that initiate meridians through the arms into the head and trunk. Each finger also corresponds to one of the five elements that make up our world (see chart on page 69). Thus, if you hurt a finger, you could discover its message by considering the energy of that element and its corresponding meridian. For example, the little finger is the element of earth and the source point of the heart meridian. Your heart might be needing some mineral or earth essence to maintain its balance. By meditating or imagining the earth nourishing you, the energies would prevent further imbalance to your body as a whole.

TRUNK:

Holds the inner organs that nourish the body and protect its functions.

LUNGS:

Relate to the fear of being in body. The lungs store anxiety. They bring the breath of life to the body. Each lung is divided into three lobes, which necessitate a different kind of breathing. As you master true breath, you will find that your body is under your command. For example, if you are afraid or angry, you will notice that you are breathing in short, shallow breaths. By breathing from the bottom lobe in full deep breaths, you will totally change your bodily response so that the fear or anger passes.

HEART:

The heart is the very center of the body's purpose and function. Earth is the planet of the heart chakra where the lessons of compassion and love are major themes. Heart trouble is always the result of emotional conflict in terms of self-nourishment and worth. Anger and fear both cause a squeezing of the heart that constricts the vessels and prompts further imbalance. You can learn to open the heart both physically and spiritually.

PANCREAS:

Balances blood sugar. Hypoglycemia and hyperglycemia are both symbolic of themes about receiving love.

STOMACH:

Where we break down food and life so we can assimilate them. If we can't "stomach" life, we will suffer from heartburn and acid stomach. Chinese medicine treats mental disease through the stomach. The stomach or solar plexus is the center of nourishment for the emotions. In truth, we *perceive the world* through this area.

GALLBLADDER:

"Official in charge of decisions." Displaced pain behind the left shoulder is often related to gallbladder blockage due to indecision. Holding back and not making the choice necessary for growth will trigger the formation of gallstones.

LIVER:

"The official in charge of the chi/energy." Stores energy in the form of glycogen, which is broken down into quick sugar for action. Anger is also held in the liver. The eyes correspond to the liver. Eye problems indicate liver themes. Pain behind the right shoulder blade (scapula) reflexes to the liver. The liver is the organ of purification: physiologically, emotionally, spiritually.

SPLEEN:

Holds old anger from other incarnations. It also is a major site for red blood production and immune support. The spleen gives us a great message: from the old and negative comes the new and vital. When the spleen is removed, it is imperative to maintain a positive approach to life.

SMALL INTESTINE:

Where we assimilate our food. Very susceptible to parasitic invasion, which has to do with allowing negative forces to overpower us. In Chinese medicine, "the official in charge of separating the pure from the impure." This not only refers to food, but to everything in our lives. If you have problems here, you may be working on receiving and worthiness. The theme of an ectomorph body type is typical of this hyperactive style, not allowing much input and not nourishing the self. Drugs such as antibiotics and marijuana are stored in this region of the body. If you have abdominal bloating in the afternoon, the flora and fauna of this area need to be re-balanced with acidophilus and other intestinal friendly organisms.

LARGE INTESTINE:

Organ of elimination. Colicky colon, constipation, and other disturbances of the large intestine are the result of prolonged anxiety states, which disrupt the whole digestive process. Gas, sometimes accompanied by headaches, may indicate the presence of "evil chi" (or bad energy) in the colon, which might be coming from others around you (as is the case with those studying the healing professions who initially tend to take on negativity to help others). Fear energy causes the primordial body to prepare for "flight or fight," at the expense of digestion. The large intestine is where we hold grief. Because guilt and shame are often associated with grief, we may find them there as well. As with the small intestine, spectrabiotics (which contain several "good guy" organisms) can help you create an environment in which evil chi or bad bacteria simply cannot exist.

KIDNEYS:

Filter out the unwanted substances from the fluid systems of the body. The kidneys are the deepest organs of the body energetically, and nourish the heart energy. They represent our ancestral chi, which we inherit from our blood relatives. Deep residues of fear pool in the kidneys, where they may eventually form kidney stones. The right kidney holds fear related to yang or masculine expression. The left kidney expresses yin or feminine fear themes.

BLADDER:

Where we hold tears. As we dream to release our emotional and psychic stress, the bladder fills up and wants to be relieved at night. It reacts the same way during the day when we want to escape anxiety-provoking situations.

SEXUAL ORGANS/GONADS:

Much of our sense of self is based on our sexual experience. The gonads are the organs of reproduction and, as such, carry us through the great transitions of life: from childhood to adulthood at puberty, and the menopause (for women). Infections of the vagina, uterus, tubes, and prostrate imply disharmony of a sexual nature, definitely involving hidden guilt.

BREASTS:

Are symbolic of nurturing. The increase in breast cancer today is directly related to the bodily confusion from going beyond physical nurturing in a world where a woman may choose to nurture an idea, rather than a child. It is crucial to communicate to your body that the essence of nurturing can be transmitted by the breasts into many aspects of life and thereby not lost. Women very much need to learn to nurture themselves.

SPINE:

Holds the body erect. Problems at specific levels correspond to different organs. Most significant is the lower back, which has to do with the holding of sexual energy.

HIPS:

Where we hold power and the precious source of life (in the genitals and base of the spine). As we feel that it erodes away, so often do our hips. Use visualization techniques to bathe your hip joints with the juice of synovial fluid that keeps you flexible and strong.

LEGS:

Provide the movement we need for growth. Thus, any trouble in your legs suggests fear of change or of moving forward in your life.

THIGHS:

The outer thighs reflex to the intestines. When the thighs are fleshy with "saddle bags," there is an indication of sluggishness on the part of the endocrine glands. The inner thighs hold sexual anger.

KNEES:

Speak about our continued flexibility on all levels. We must be able to stretch on mental as well as physical levels. We hold karma in the knees, and that binding energy often keeps us from moving forward.

ANKLES:

Necessitate great flexibility to move in any direction. We sprain that ankle when we are uncertain of our capacity to try something new. Hesitation blocks new energy.

FEET:

Plant us firmly on this Planet Earth. Through them we take the necessary steps. The feet are the negative pole of the body, allowing us to discharge negative energy. The left foot has to do with receiving and the right foot with visibility and doing.

SKELETON:

Is the support system of the body, while the bone marrow is central to our bodily defenses through the production of white corpuscles. Problems in the bones or skeletal system have to do with conflicts about being in body and the feeling of lack of support.

SKIN:

The skin is the largest organ of elimination. Eruptions of the skin indicate that the blood is overloaded with toxins and the body is trying to rid itself of impurities. Often, the body is trying to tell us about something it cannot tolerate.

Consider each and all imbalances, accidents, and illnesses you have experienced in your body and review them in terms of this symbolic code. Contemplate what was happening to you at the time and see if it illuminates the purposes of the experience. You can also find broad sweeps of themes laid down in any part of your body, corresponding to your own body's infinite repertoire.

You can greatly quicken the pace of your spiritual growth by using your body as the tool for releasing the themes that crop up on a daily basis. One day you may run the gamut from jealousy to abundance. Work with each one as a theme you can access energetically in your body. Just as you did with love in the previous chapter, "The Body Speaks," ask your body where it is holding the energy of [love, abundance, power, and so forth] and when you find it, free it to course through your entire body. If the theme is a negative one (such as jealousy, regret, resentment, anger, or fear), find where your body is holding it and ask what color is needed to dissolve and release it. Take the first color (or colors) that comes into your consciousness; imagine you are taking it into the place your body is holding the theme and allow the color to free you from that energy. You will be astounded at how quickly and profoundly this works.

The purpose of this kind of exercise in consciousness is to become aware that your body is indeed speaking to you and help-ing you to receive the teachings being given by the Soul. Your body has been willing to bear the pain and discomfort in order to focus your attention on its symbolic themes. It never does these things on its own, or to punish you, but rather as a conversation with you on its deepest levels. The direction of bodily energy is always towards health and homeostasis.

We are very close to a new octave of existence in which disease and death will no longer be a part of our bodily expression. These new realities await our further spiritual maturation and the lessons we are experiencing now, which further our growth. Residues from other incarnations are locked within the mind of our cells and require release; the pains and deaths of those bodies are reflected in the bodies we carry now.

BASIC FACE TYPES

Most of us are a combination of these features. See which one most closely fits you.

THE SQUARE FACE: *Provides the sturdy, basic, down to earth focus. Can be too rigid or stern.*

THE HEART-SHAPED FACE: *Sometimes wider at the top, lending a focus to mental faculties. Provides the use of energies from the galactic and devic kingdoms. Can be an impish personality, but also difficult to deal with. Often the ears are set on an angle, lending galactic influence and making the themes more intricate.*

THE ROUND FACE: *Open. The theme relates to the mastery of emotional energies.*

THE OVAL-SHAPED FACE: *the width is greatest in the middle, lending a strong physical quality.*

THE LONG, RECTANGULAR FACE: *This is the galactic face. It is angular. We jokingly call it the "cookie cutter" face, because it could have been cut out of a mold. It is often accompanied by "galactic" ears and other features that make the person appear otherworldly.*

Classic Square Face

**Classic Devic Heart-shaped Face
with Galactic Ears**

**Devic Heart-Shaped Face
with Devic Ears**

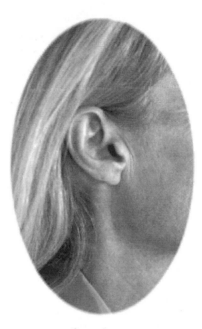

Galactic Ears

**Galactic "Cookie Cutter" —
Rectangular Face with Galactic Ears**

Oval Devic Face

Angelic Round Face

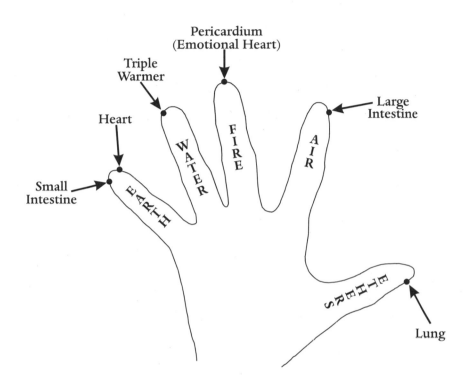

**ACUPUNCTURE MERIDIANS AND ELEMENTS
REPRESENTED IN THE FINGERS**

THEME BODIES

The form of the body expresses the themes of the Soul by developing attributes that allow it to carry out its activities in relationship to the lessons the Soul has designed for any one lifetime. Not only does the Soul deposit the seeds of its teachings in specific parts of the body, but the body mold itself carries the shapes and characteristics of lifetimes experienced in different cultures and races, as well as in the present physical DNA. The body seems to call out its predilections and creates an individual composition even beyond its physical inheritance, based on its peculiar destiny.

People will often survey a body and comment upon its purpose or capabilities merely by looking at its shape.

"That little boy is built for speed," they'll say.

"Look at those hips. She's just made for having babies!"

Indeed, they are right. The body weaves purpose into all its designs. The shape of a body is not the product of physical inheritance alone, but rather is built for specific functions, related to themes that are carried over from cultural and spiritual contexts. We can imagine carrying the genetic material of our forefathers, but we don't realize that their thoughts, feelings, and experiential conclusions are tucked away inside us as well. Their adaptability to their environment was whispered along the double helixes into our bones and breasts to help our bodies perform better or, less fortunately, causing us to repeat the same lessons.

Spiritually, we choose our parents. We choose them not only for the kind of relationship they will engage in with us, but also for the physical, cultural, and societal challenges they will present to us. We may be learning mainly from their cultural channels, as well as their physical channels. This is why we so often feel that we are different or don't belong to our families. Our body composition and personality may be heavily weighted with leftovers from other important embodiments that we must access and utilize to fulfill our destiny.

There are many diseases today which are thought to have a propensity to be inherited. Some are faulty genetic encoding. It would help our understanding of these mechanisms immeasurably if we recognized that genetic inheritance may also be the result of emotional, familial, and cultural similarities brought about by karmic contracts. Thus, a familial disease may have to do with a common theme or contract shared by a family. For example, heart disease is thought to be passed down in families. Heart trouble may be caused by emotional constriction in which we actually squeeze the heart by holding so tightly to hurts and angers. I observe that people with heart trouble have very discolored pericardial fluids, which are the liquids that actually surround the heart and provide a protective cushion within the pericardial sac. If a parent has learned to "hold the heart," s/he will unwittingly teach that attitude or behavior to the children.

Diabetes is another disease that seems to be involved in inherited relationships. As a body theme, it relates to giving and receiving love, the "sweet" force in our life. Sugar is also the source of bodily energy and therefore suggests the theme of fear of being in body. Since sugar is symbolic of that loving energy for life, the inability to control or balance it speaks of family karma in terms of relationship themes. Diabetes usually necessitates a great deal of family participation in its process and thereby allows the whole family to work on the karmic theme together.

Breast cancer is a disease with a distinct theme about nurturing. The breasts are the primordial symbols of safety, comfort, and nurturing — both giving the nurturing and receiving it. Many women develop breast cancer when their children are gone; they feel emotionally that they can no longer fulfill that role and are set adrift from their sense of themselves. Conversely, many younger women experience lumps, cysts, and even breast cancer, related to the fact that they are choosing to not use their bodies for that direct form of nurturing. The physical body needs to understand that this intrinsic element is not atrophied, but can be expressed by her capacity to nurture a business or a nation, and to do it with her voice, her thoughts, or even her meditations (which are symbolic of that same energy). She must also experience the nurturing energies that she can direct towards her own self. The breasts are depositories and channels for this essential energy, which can be translated into many forms and frequencies.

As we learn more about the subtle body pathways and encodings that shape us, we will be able to track the effects of thoughts and even such a vague correlation as cultural adaptations on body form and style. Though we may initially surmise that it is a "chicken and the egg" effect, in terms of whether the physical genetic component came first or the cultural aptitudes formed a commonality in terms of shape and gesture, it is hard to determine. That they exist is undeniable. I can often tell where a person is from, simply by observing the way they "stand" in their body, which reflects deeply rooted familial and inherited cultural patterns. We must begin to recognize that inheritance is branded into our beingness on societal and cultural levels, and that these tendencies are expressed through physical form.

If we explore beyond the physical blueprints, we will always discover the collective and cultural patterns that underlie them. They can be recognized as broad, thematic expressions that encompass wide strokes of life perspectives.

Long ago, when we existed mostly as wandering tribes, our themes were perhaps more homogeneous than in present day. We sought shelter, food, and safety. Physical characteristics of height, density, and even coloring were forged by the primordial body's survival mechanisms within the demands of the immediate environment.

We multiplied and became more stable as a species, and began to orient ourselves within mythologies that expressed our sense of ourselves in the great scheme of things. We developed "cultural" perspectives that prescribed how we carried out our lives. As we added symbolic reality to our experience, we found the purpose of our existence in acts of more and more specific cultural relativity.

The Soul has an interactive circle of connecting angles to describe a theme and its variations. The society, culture, race, community, family, gender, and position in the family — each provides aspects that enhance the expression of a theme.

Our diversified cultures have come to express Soul themes through concepts of societal values. For example, different cultures value women at specific societal levels, within well defined behavioral contexts. The "place" of a woman in her home and cultural environment can be observed in the way she carries her body. She will exhibit subtle cues as to how she feels about herself and her worth by the way she carries her head and the angle of her shoulders, her body stance, and especially the expressions of her face and eyes. Even though she will have copied most of her gestures from other female models around her, the deep sense of value or power that is hers alone will be palpable. If you placed three females in a family side by side, you would be able to discern the order of their place by these subtle, yet clearly presented body postures.

Our blood inheritance influences these bodily patterns (expressed through cultural characteristics), and is visible to the discerning eye. Thus, a person might belong to a German culture by virtue of birth and yet exhibit very "Swiss" characteristics because of a grandparent who was of Swiss blood; an American can be "very Italian," by virtue of blood and cultural inheritance.

If someone were to ask you what blood lines you carry, you might answer, "French and Italian," "Scotch-Irish," "African," "Latin," or "Asian." Some parts of the world hold cultures and races very separate from each other, while others (like America) are great genetic and cultural melting pots. I, for example, am a mixture of seven different ethnic groups and each one has left an indelible mark on my being, even though I have never visited some of those places or people.

In one of my classes at The Nizhoni School for Global Consciousness, we studied each other's features relative to our blood lines. It was fascinating to see how perceptive the students were in isolating physical characteristics that corresponded to the blood factors. There were recognizable commonalties in features such as "Polish eyes," "Roman legs" and "Dutch foreheads." It was incredible to look at the body as a whole and see so many attributes of different blood lines all visible in the same body. Sometimes it was not just the shape, but also the way the body moved or used a part that gave it its cultural distinction.

I remember a story about an American spy in Russia who had succeeded in penetrating into the inner circle until one night, under the influence of a great deal of vodka, he unconsciously picked up his fork in the American way and was shot dead, right there and then. He had betrayed himself by a subtle but alien gesture that could not have been performed by a "true" Russian.

It is unfathomable to imagine how many gestures and nuances lie tucked away in the mind of the cells, remembered not by verbal or physical coaching, but by blood memories alone. Countless times, families have approached me to whisper in awe that they are sure someone who had died has reincarnated again as a child in the same family. They report that the child subsequently makes the same gestures as the deceased, without ever having met him or her. Often, the child will have the same likes and dislikes, habits, and special talents as did the other. Could it be? Absolutely! This is also true, however, of children who have never been exposed to one of their parents and yet walk in exactly the same manner or hold other identical characteristics. It comes from the inextricable link that is passed between bodies of the One Soul.

The gestures, postures, the strengths, weaknesses, and composition of the parts are all elements of the body's magnificent story. It is the story of the Soul, told through the specific focus of its themes. By virtue of its thematic focus, the Soul hones itself into an instrument of creation.

You may ask, "What is my life's purpose?" If you explore your experiences through the lens of themes, you will be able to see that whatever actions you engage in must be a part of mastering those themes. From this perspective, you can never make a "mistake," because everything about you is always in the context of those teachings emanating from your Soul. There are probably some kinds of work or activities that you are deeply drawn to doing. Often these are memories of skills or themes you have been working on in other incarnations. That is why you may feel unfulfilled or numbed once you actually begin doing them, because they bring you back to a repetition filled with karma.

In truth, what you do is irrelevant. It is the consciousness with which you do it that makes the difference. Perhaps you have a rather monotonous job. However, it may be offering you the opportunity to function on many levels at once. The theme may relate to helping others, creating an ambiance that deeply influences their lives. You may be learning patience, compassion, creativity, or intuition.

Ask inside, to your Higher Self, regarding the theme of your work or activities. Don't try to think up the answer; just allow it to come to you spontaneously. Once you recognize it, you will find that you can enjoy your work more because you will see it in a different light. Sometimes that recognition alone can give you the courage to change your job and move on to new challenges, without fear!

We are often drawn to activities that will help us heal ourselves. For example, a teacher who has had a terrible childhood may choose teaching in an attempt to heal those early experiences by affecting the lives of children. Healers often become healers to re-balance karmic debts they have to others they have harmed in other lifetimes. It is a perfect symbiotic choice, that helps us to see the web of our intertwining lives.

Can you imagine yourself a body of themes? Usually the central themes of our lives are the ones we resist the most. I call it the "blind spot": the veil through which we cannot see truth. It is a form of teaching that is often difficult, yet illuminating. My Higher Self says, "Whatever you resist, that's what you get!"

It means that you will be entrapped by whatever you hold away from you, until you can release it by mastering its theme — until it passes through you without harm or resistance.

You can use your body to penetrate that veil of resistance.

Think for a minute about a part of your body that you feel is disconnected or out of balance with the rest of you. If there is any bodily feature or part that stands out, it very definitely will be holding a clue to some central theme. Usually you will reject this part of your body and not give it any guidance, love, or acceptance because you do not want to acknowledge it. Yet it is a most important part of you because it holds the secrets of your growth.

It may be a shape that has lingered from another incarnational experience and so all unconscious association with it creates a block in you. This is why it is so important to consciously clear your incarnations of the Soul, as we do at The Light Institute. Since the body is symbolic even in its shape and form, you can glean a great deal of awareness by allowing it to show you the meaning of its symbology.

During my workshops on the theme of Soul Bodies, we always explore these body encapsulations to find out what they might offer us to transmute or uphold. Once we can make the connection, we ask the body to show us the source and purpose of its design. This goes a long way to help people accept their bodies as they are, without so much judgment and even to admire them from a new perspective. Often the body will show you how you have chosen a form you used successfully in another life that will support you now. It may repeat that form again, giving you the opportunity to continue working on that particular theme.

Sometimes you choose a loathsome body expressly to learn how to love it as it is. A woman who is very fat and heavy, for example, may choose such a body because in a former beautiful body, she created karma by misusing her body or losing herself in the physical. The plump body is the classical endomorph of intuitive people who hold their power energetically in their bodies. Such recognition has a great deal to teach one about a deeper relationship with their body. In Rubens' time, a plump body would have been the desirable feminine form and this could be the body's purpose for restructuring itself now as it was then. Think how confusing it is to the body to be received in an abhorrent fashion after having been so adored before! Only your body knows the source of its predilections. All you have to do is ask it.

Here are some examples from the workshops that I especially love:

(A woman with thin, very fine hair)

"I see that I am of the fairy kingdom. My whole body is so delicate and refined. It's like gossamer and my hair is wispy and beautiful as well."

(A teenage girl with a rounded hip area and small breasts)

"I am a mermaid. I can feel myself sitting on the rocks and also moving through the water with my strong fish-like tail. I am very beautiful. Maybe my shape isn't so bad after all!"

(A teenage boy who is very small for his age)

"*I am an Egyptian architect who has designed the great pyramid at Cheops. I am even a little taller than the pharaoh. I can see the passageways behind me which match my perfect height. I am very successful and feel powerful in my body.*"

(A fat man)

"*I see an African woman with large buttocks. She is doing a kind of belly dance and enjoying herself. Its a very sensual and I can feel it in my body too. I love it!*"

(A woman with large thighs)

"*I see a Trojan warrior. Very strong and powerful through the legs. ... I like the sense of his power.*"

You could try this exercise too:

Bring your consciousness into a meditative state by breathing deeply until you feel very relaxed.

Focus your awareness into the place in your body that you don't like.

Ask your body to show you another body that is encapsulated there from other cultures or races that authored the shape you have now.

Just allow yourself to imagine what is there. Take the first flicker that comes to you. You may see or feel or hear the presence of this other body.

When you perceive it, let yourself experience that body completely to know the advantages it provided you through its form.

Now, ask your body what color it needs to release the other body.

Draw the color or colors into your body, into the place you are working on, and allow the color to wash away the residues of that other body.

When you feel that it is gone, breathe deeply and open your eyes.

If you feel there are several places that don't fit with the form of your overall body, do the exercise in each place to see where they came from. You will find this fascinating and exceedingly helpful to view yourself in a new way. Some of the images will bring you a sense of humor, which is a necessary part of self-awareness and acceptance.

Sometimes it isn't just a part of the body, but rather whole segments of the body that seem discountenant. For example, it is common to see that the bottom half of the body is very masculine and the top half is feminine. It might be entirely the other way around, in which the top is very strong or developed and the bottom is weak. Though you are half male, half female, it seems a trick of fate to be composed in such an obvious way. It does, however, tell you that you have a theme concerning the yin/yang balance of your essence. Sometimes it is as if the body is split down the middle and the left side (which represents the yin or feminine) and the right side (the yang or masculine) are very different. The different sides of the face are often dissimilar, as well. If your body is composed in any of these ways, it is expressing to you the importance of integrating your masculine/feminine energies.

If you find that you always hurt the same side of the body, you can be sure that it is showing you a relationship to the yin/yang theme. The body is crying out for your attention to the energies stored in those areas. The yin (left) side represents the internal, hidden, feminine qualities and the yang (right) side expresses the external, manifestation attributes of the masculine. You can work on this re-balancing through your inner essences of Inner Male and Inner Female and you will feel a dramatic change in your beingness. I have spoken about this at length in my book, *Feminine Fusion*. Multi-incarnational work is profoundly helpful to clarify the significant bodies you have retained within your repertoire, corresponding to the male/female themes.

Some cultures express a predominately yang or yin energetic within their societal living styles. The Romans, Vikings, Atlanteans, galactics, Mongols, and perhaps even the Americans up until now, could be viewed as decidedly yang because of their focus on the external world. India, Tibet, Indonesia, and most island cultures, as well as the angelic and devic realms, offer the yin perspective of value placed on the inner or invisible worlds.

Every person on this planet has experienced all races, as well as both male and female incarnations. Our genetic pool extends out to the forty-fourth cousin, which means we are very closely related as a species, despite some people's fervent denial of that fact. Only the thoughtforms set forth by our diverse cultural mandates cause us to cling to the tragic illusion that we cannot find oneness.

Though it would seem too stereotypical to clump body types into racial or cultural categories alone, physical anthropologists and anatomists have measured and delineated specific attributes of the five major races which might well correspond to their evolutionary environment. Even without all that knowledge, we can decipher the echoes of those body types for ourselves, if we care to explore our rich human heritage. There are certain nuances, profiles, and inflections that give us cues as to one's birthrights, whether they are multi-incarnational or blood-related.

My students and I reviewed the various bodies we wore in different lifetimes to see how they are mirrored in us now. It was truly astonishing to discover how easily they could be recognized. Up came the Indians, Mongols, Africans, Lemurians, and Druids, by just a shape of the eye, the turn of a hip, the length of the fingers. Each and all homogenous groups have traits that describe them, is also illuminating to consider how the body "housing" guards and enhances the themes that are relevant to any group.

You may be wondering why you would want to relate to other bodies, or you may even feel very resistant to the whole idea. Those negative feelings actually come from conclusions you have drawn from your incarnational experiences. You may feel negatively about another culture because of carryover memories in which you were enemies with that group, or you may have suffered and died as a result of being from that culture yourself. Those imprints are within the mind of the cell and definitely influence our irrational feelings about others. As a Soul group, we cannot afford to carry these energies into the future.

Think about the bodies you saw in the exercise and see what comes to you about the themes of those experiences. In general, it is very illuminating to view experience from the perspective of themes. For example, if you have a negative habit, look at the theme it is expressing and you will find the clarity to stop repeating it. If you are having trouble in relationships, contemplate the major themes you encounter through them and work on the theme, rather than the relationship, per se. The theme might be dependency, projection, freedom, loyalty, or jealousy. The truth is that until you release those themes, you will probably only pick partners who will repeat them with you. It is not the partner, it is the theme!

If we take a small sojourn around the planet and across time, we can study ourselves by discussing some of our ancestors, in terms of their general overall themes. Many cultures based their life patterns on spiritual or mystical expressions that gave purpose to their existence. It was essential to find a place for themselves within the infinite scope of the universe. They found the explanation of all things through creating cohesive mappings of interconnectedness. They described human purpose through their relationship to the elements, the spirit of all things, the mysteries — which they named and with which they set up elaborate symbolic and ritualistic forms of communication. They based their reality upon their relationship to the gods and the mysteries of unseen worlds.

The Atlantean culture has been the genesis of many civilizations. They left their mark more than 50,000 years ago. The Atlanteans communicated with beings from around the cosmos and though they were more focused on the galactic aspects of technology and the theme of manifestation, they originated what later civilizations concluded were gods, through their manipulation of genetic pools and their capacity to actually design new species. They played with combining genetic material and created such beings as the centaurs, the Pegasus, and many more, who became the creatures we know of through Greek mythology.

The Atlanteans interfaced with giants and Cyclopes and other "experiments" of their own making and those sent from other parts of the galaxy, before overstepping their place and destroying themselves. Just prior to that cataclysmic event, some Atlanteans migrated to other continents and seeded future cultures. Their exodus quickened the Egyptians, Hindus, and Mayans, who later passed down to the Greeks, Romans, Incas, and Aztecs the mythologies born of Atlantean experience.

The Egyptians developed their strength through levels of awareness pertaining to other dimensions and even other worlds. There can be no doubt that they were influenced by beings from beyond Earth, as were the Atlanteans. They used their light, small bodies to help them travel through the underworlds and beyond.

The Egyptians and the Mayans both sought to alter the shape of their heads to mirror some form they perceived as having spiritual attributes through those specific body shapes and features. They used external measures to slant the forehead and back of the head (to enhance the "enlightened" powers of the priesthood), perhaps to copy what they had seen elsewhere.

It was not just "Gods and Galactics" that we inherited from the Atlanteans; we also have inherited their central theme of the use of power. Along with splitting the androgynous body into separate male and female parts, they became focused on individual will. The Atlanteans discovered the challenge of personal power. They misused it and today we are enmeshed in the very same point of choice that was presented to them. Hopefully, we will choose Spock's axiom "the good of the whole," rather than "the good of the one," and come to recognize that we must work together. It is too late for the old "King of the Mountain" game on our planet. There is another way.

The Romans brought the game of power down into the physical realm. They had bodies made for carrying heavy armor, with thick legs capable of marching and conquering. If you have these physical attributes, consider what you might learn about the art of conquering now, and how to express that very yang/masculine energy in a way that really serves the whole. The Romans utilized the yang elements of manifestation and structure to build government and human law as a way of focusing life and culture.

Through their philosophies, the Chinese also created laws of living and used them for divine inspiration. Both the Chinese and the Tibetans were influenced by the Lemurians, who had a very advanced civilization with a magnificent social structure that predated the Atlanteans.

There are more esoteric theme bodies to contemplate that speak of our relationship to other worlds and realities. The heart-shaped face of the devic kingdom that represents the nature spirits can be seen in all cultures. The angelic realm holds profound teaching about unconditional love, visibility, and patience. The various "races" of angelics are quite discernible to us. There are many variations of the galactic themes which might be hinted at by the slant, size, and shape of the ears. The galactics inspire our admiration of their advanced technology and mirror our own dilemma of discovering the connecting link between technology and the spiritual realms.

TREADING LIVES

I know that you must have had moments in your life in which you felt unable to be completely present in the here and now, or even in your body. Sometimes it is just too hard to face the difficulties and the decisions that cry out to us so relentlessly. The daily flood of choices and information is often quite overwhelming. It is then that the numbing effects of "suspended animation" kick in and you just allow the blurring field of vision to sweep past you. It is a kind of state I call "automatic pilot." It is just functional enough to get by on, but certainly it is not a part of true life which pokes and prods the skin of your memory, bringing you endlessly to the mirror of all clarity, from which you return to your own image in trance.

If you have not asked yourself what your life is about, you cannot possibly fathom how you might use it. You may feel that life is using you. In truth, the whole universe is using you. It is using you as an experiment of Divine expression. Could you imagine the possibility that you exist throughout the universe? Certainly the human form is not universal, but the universal essence is, at least in part, human. Essence is essential to life. Essence need not take on a body, but a body cannot exist without an essence. Your body is rich in Divine essence awaiting your awareness.

There are infinite ways to distract yourself from the essential questions: through relationships and illusions, material things and dreams. All of the diversions may give you a sense of treading water and that all of your activities accomplish nothing but to keep you afloat. You are suspended here, waiting for something you can't remember to happen or return. In fact, you are waiting for critical mass to occur, in which all the necessary elements come together to cause a change, an evolution of any situation, or of your beingness itself. From the outer perspective, it is impossible to witness the forces at play that bring the energies together, yet they are palpable in the pregnant void of consciousness. You know something will happen, but you do not realize that as you are waiting for it, it is waiting for you!

In the last few days or even moments before death, I have heard people say, "I have waited my whole life for this!"

They are speaking of the illumination that showers down on them when their ego is no longer protecting them from truth. They have relinquished the struggle to tread the water of their lives and are now simply floating in the memories and experiences that have buoyed them throughout this embodiment. Close to the end, the dying move in and out of their bodies as if practicing death. They are accessing the energies of other dimensions which are a part of who they are, in terms of a Soul on its journey of evolution.

As things move more swiftly, there is a juxtaposition of time and space and suddenly life begins to be perceived as simultaneous. This is why we have the feeling that the light comes to get us and carry us off. In reality, it is that we break through the veil to experience the light that has always been there with us, simultaneously in this existence.

We do have the capacity to live simultaneous realities; in fact, most of us are doing so now. It is not such a difficult concept if you contemplate the cosmic law that the body follows the mind. As the mind conceives, the body enacts. Imagine the infinite Soul placing a particle spark of its whole into a body. It can place sparks in any direction and in any other body in this same flicker. The Soul engages in simultaneous lifetimes because they are a more holographic way of learning; it can practice a theme from all around the circle. For example, the human body can extend itself back to Divine awareness by practicing the angelic axioms of unconditional love and compassion, while the angelic body can anchor the cosmic frequencies by connecting to physical form and learning more about human dynamics, so as to be of better service while strengthening the human seed with its angelic encoding.

Simultaneous lifetimes are an excellent balance to the interface between worlds and have become a major incarnational pattern, specific to this point of Earth evolution. There are many angel/humans on the planet at this time. Perhaps you are one of them.

The difficulty of simultaneity lies in the necessity of bringing the two simultaneous frequencies together so that they can support one another, rather than each struggling to be expressed independently. Instead of the potential ecstasy they offer, you might actually be suffering because you are not aware of this arrangement and so feel as if you are a misfit in some strange and inexplicable way. There is a fascination and longing to be attached to these higher frequencies and, simultaneously, a depreciation of the human experience.

Are you a dreamer who appears to be incapable of getting on with your life? You might be unconsciously dealing with simultaneous existence by developing a kind of seesaw effect in your consciousness. One minute you are here and then you feel very removed, as if listening to some other reality. Of course you actually are tuned in to someplace else, but the only way you access it is by daydreaming in suspended animation.

Simultaneous lifetimes are not an excuse for avoiding responsibility; they necessitate even more commitment to serving one's purpose within a greater whole. When you discover that you are having a simultaneous lifetime and the veil between them is removed, there is a great surge of energy as the two separate lives rush together in a spectacular fusion of energies.

At The Light Institute, when a simultaneous lifetime is uncovered, we very carefully weave the two existences together so that the person becomes more integrated into this body. Each simultaneous lifetime has a "spin point," through which its energies affect this body. Once we locate this spin point, you can begin to consciously participate in the sharing of energies between the two lives. If you need information or a special frequency which is available from your simultaneous lifetime, you can access it through the spin point. In like manner, human information can be extended to increase the understanding between dimensions and species, as you perform the valuable task of the intermediary.

When the simultaneous lifetime is one of Divine stature, The Light Institute facilitator will also open the DNA to activate and amplify its role within the mind of the cell. When you have discovered the larger hologram of your existence, you will find a great peace in the synthesis of such expanded arenas.

Many simultaneous lifetimes are connected to dimensions such as the astral and other dimensions, where existence transcends the arch of time. The consciousness of one body can coalesce into a being who may incarnate several times in different bodies, while still connected to the same simultaneous "partner" lifetime in the timeless dimension. This is true of galactic lifetimes, which may continue beyond the existence of the Earth body because of the difference in galactic and human time frames.

Here is the story of a wonderful and gentle man who has been caught in a cosmic commitment of great service, but which ultimately has necessitated his reclaiming his human body:

"It is a long time ago in Earth time. I am a small energy flying through the galaxy. There is great peace within my being, which is a sky blue color in the rough outline and shape of a four-year-old boy. I am very wise, yet innocent, and also very old."

It is significant to add here that in this present lifetime he discovered how to shift dimensions at the age of four years old.

"I wanted to play, to expand. I focused my great intent and just slipped out into space. ... It was so free and joyous, yet I felt that I was sneaking away from my body."

"I was home in the stars, surrounded by light, and the universe was sprinkled with billions of sparkling diamonds. I could feel the heart beat of God pulsing through everything. I looked back down at my human body and could feel the tension and intensity of not being comfortable in its form.

"I continued to play in the playground of the cosmos, yet in the background of my being I felt a knowing that I should go back, that it is wrong to be here now. ... Some other star children come along to play, but I have to go back; I cannot play.

"I have a job to do back on Earth; it is to raise the light in people.

"When I hear this, I no longer feel burdened, as I know my time will come when I can rest and play. I see my crystal Light Body merge with my body and emit a powerful blue light. ... At the point of their integration, I remember that the light is within, and the time is now!

"As I am flowing along in space, I hear a calling that is echoing like ripples across the cosmos. It comes from the God Source and is sent out by the Great Council of all galactics: 'There is an experiment going on Earth and we need volunteers to come forth.'

"Immediately I knew I had to go. I felt that there would not be many beings able enough for this mission. I had the knowing that I had previously gone forth on other callings into other dimensions to be a trumpeter of change, an observer, and relayer back to the Council. In truth, I am an experiment created by the galactic Council — a human with a galactic shield. I will hold the light and be the window into the human sky through which the galactics can view the human experiment.

"The first episode begins with walking down a metal staircase inside a cave that leads me into the Earth. At the end of a platform, human people are standing, waiting. They are awake but appear to be in a trance.

"I go up and stand just to the side of them. I emit a blue light and let them know that I will show them how to get to other dimensions and where they should go next. "It is as if they are being reminded or re-awakened, so they can remember how to move on.

"A blue light vessel comes and I go back and forth from Earth to other dimensions, shuttling the people and reassuring them that all is well. I have the ability to break through the dimensions without effort.

"The next lifetime I land in the twelfth century trying to hold the light. ... I am a knight, resplendent in my armor, riding on a magnificent horse, upright and staunch.

"There is a light coming down from the heavens that wavers at the top of my golden and silver chakras. I am the grounding element of this light on the planet.

"Around me there is war going on. A fog covers the land and muffles the cries of the dying and the clashing of swords. I am peaceful amongst the chaos. I am holding the sword of God firmly within. The message it speaks is that it is time for everyone to awaken.

"Angels are carrying the dead bodies up into the sky ever so swiftly but gently and without comment or judgment. There is great sadness

*for the carnage they see. When, at last, I am released from that life-
time, my consciousness carries the residue of the earthly reality and
experiences. I feel all the pain and now I feel human anger towards the
council because they cannot share what it is like to have an emotional
body. I understand that the council wants to learn from our experiences, but I am caught between these two worlds.*

"My body is protected by a galactic silver energy that emanates
around my armor. I am human with a galactic silver suit. It is as if
the two bodies have merged their essence into one.

"The human form pulses of compassion and in the center of this
combination of form is a vibrant heart. The galactic form shines of
protection and higher knowing. It manifests itself in this body as the
silver armor.

"This lifetime I have created a body of human and galactic heritage: human heart, galactic energy. I serve as a vessel on Earth for
others to see what it is like here. I feel connected to everyone and everything.

"There is a third lifetime, in which I am a soldier in the muddy
trenches in France during World War I. Once again I am an observer,
as I hold the connection of light from the Council of Galactics. Only
now I hide the light, as it has caused too much deep pain from being
caught between these two realities. My head begins to pound as the
galactics and their light try to come in through me and into the density of my body. I feel that they are all trying to cram inside me and see
what is going on. I am being invaded and have too little space for myself.

"The Galactic Council pushes me to look closer at what is happening and I can't help but take on the emotional fear of the dying into

my body, which is now very heavy. The Galactic Council had implanted me with the ability to take on the negative and dark forces into my emotional body so that I could transform it. Like an alchemist, I am to shift the lower energies into the light. This is their experiment for which I am the prototype.

"I choose to die. As my light releases from my body, an Alien appears at my side and tries to reach into my solar plexus to get my light. Not all galactic species work within the light. I hold open a space from my dying body and extend myself upwards, out of the third dimension, and expand to all of the other galactic dimensions.

"I feel stretched, aware of all levels of existence. It is as if I am a whirlwind spinning through the universe, speaking the message to not let this happen. The vortex of human/galactic I have become carries the emotions and vibrations of killing and warfare. I am trying to show all the galactic species what it means and more importantly, how it feels. I hear my inner voice saying to the galactics swarming around me, 'Let me do it my way now.' They must let go of us and not use us in this way as they cannot perceive the pain it causes."

To finish the session, this man did a lot of work in releasing the residues of both human pain and galactic manipulation. The contract to perform this function of being a channel between the dimensions has been released; he will carry the light visibly here and continue to commune with the Galactic Council, but from his own will and consciousness. He has reclaimed his human body from its highest potential, seeded by light.

The rewards of becoming aware of simultaneous realities could have a great effect on our willingness to use our lives on the highest octaves, while actively dissolving the social and cultural patternings that are not conducive to a peaceful future. Even the more mundane conversations about who we are expected to become, within our familial karmic bonds, must be re-balanced. I remember one woman who was a brilliant photographer and correspondent. She was the only child and struggled with a sense of duty, having not married or had children. She was lonely for relationship, yet found that she was not at all attracted to being with anyone, though she often dreamed of a gentle faraway love and the sense of children. It remained an enigma until doing sessions at The Light Institute; she discovered that she is having a simultaneous lifetime in which she has a partner and two children in another dimension, who are holding the light for her to carry out a mission of a spiritual nature here on Earth. From that point of knowing, she has begun doing spiritual work. She feels that she is receiving a wealth of loving support from that more lofty place, allowing her to fully focus her life in the inner direction.

It is time to close the gap of separation and bring ourselves into a more comprehensive universal reality, that has been going on all around us without our recognition of it. If we can find ways of bringing these frequencies into sync with our reality, we will not be so driven to choose destructive alternatives (such as alcohol and drugs) to break free from a world we cannot endure.

Drugs only lead us back into an astral soup on the dark side of karma, in which we have existed too long. There are realities of profound despair that await the space traveler who ventures out under the muse of external energies. A simultaneous experience in an interdimensional space outside of time can hold a part of the spirit captive and influence the present lifetime in a negative way. Interdimensional spaces are planes of existence in which entrapped spirits are tortured or torture others in very mechanical ways. They are a residual sleeve of the most debased galactic experiments. As purgatory is to humans, the interdimensional spaces are to galactic frequencies. Those who exist there wear a great deal of metal on their bodies. Chains and weapons form the repertoire of who they are, and there is no human emotion other than the aspect of physical pain.

There is now a dangerous bleedthrough of interdimensional energies on the planet, due to drug excess. Walk down the streets of almost any city in the world and you will see the metal and chains in full display. They say it is a fashion statement. No, it is a message about protection, by attempting to convey an illusion of power.

We have moved into an era of extremes, where the battles of light and dark going on within the cosmos are reflected here on Earth and played out, as if we are the checkerboard upon which other, more monstrous forces replay the past and stalk the future.

SCHIZOPHRENIA

There are aspects of treading lives that create struggle due to the residues of experiences that intermingle with the present reality in such a way that we cannot relate to our own self. We have discussed the validity of sourcing energetic imbalances in the residues of other lives and how, by clearing them at their source, very often the disturbances can be released. Such is the case with phobias, as we explored in the previous chapter, "The Body Speaks."

A most important example of treading lives, in terms of multi-incarnational residues, is that of schizophrenia. The person suffering under the delusions of other voices or personalities is treading the inner-dimensional spaces, where a great deal of fear-mongering takes place. Often the voices are involved in negative behavior or abusive actions for lofty causes, that range from the need for self-protection to saving the world or being the instrument of God's punishment. Indeed, I find it more than coincidental that an extremely high percentage of schizophrenics we have worked with at The Light Institute have a hidden theme of abuse in their background. Very common is sexual abuse, which casts such a thick shadow of shame that one could easily see the rationality of living through some other personality, rather than being constantly haunted by the pain of a memory, even one forcefully forgotten by the psyche. The person may choose a personality that fights back and attacks as a defense mechanism, or a paranoiac personality who sees danger in every glance and from any and all energy coming towards him or her, because of the imprint of being overwhelmed by some advancing force in the past. What has been breathtaking is the healing which takes place as the person discovers such a personality to be a body of their own that has been treading lives!

A case in point is a young woman who had eight personality appendages attached to her. She had been under psychiatric care for five years and was able to function some portion of the time through the use of special drugs that diminished her aggressiveness. She came to The Light Institute on the advice of her psychiatrist. As each personality displayed itself, the facilitator took her back to the moment she had been contacted by that voice. In each case, as we have since discovered to be predictable, the voice was another incarnation of herself. Some personalities were male and some female, with various kinds of experience in the lifetime, but all of them had an element of the theme of transgression of the self, with varying degrees of fear and shame attached to it. In her present lifetime, this woman had experienced sexual transgression in her period of puberty, less than a year before the onset of the schizophrenic episodes. Unable to assuage her shame and subsequent anger, she simply abdicated that body for one that was completely disconnected from its reality. When the sexual memories surfaced, we had to look into the purpose of the ordeal from the spiritual perspective of karma. Without the shameless clarity of spiritual understanding, it is very difficult to truly and completely release such shattering experiences.

She left The Light Institute after six sessions, a new person with an intact personality. Free from the dungeon of schizophrenia, she has remained without drugs and in healthy contact with herself for over two years. There are other such stories, so many in fact that I hope psychiatric practitioners will soon take up the tool of multi-incarnational, spiritual awareness, for the great healing potential that it truly has.

Many times when we are working with someone who feels a profound separation in his/her life, we discover that he/she cannot risk giving their "all" because not all of him/her is present. A part of them is caught in another body, whose spirit has been left outside of the evolutionary process and still whispers the repetitive vignette of its own misfortune, attracting the same into this new body by its very fixation on the other. Throughout our almost infinite incarnations, we have left an assortment of such particle spirits, which serve as tethers to our hopes and aspirations. Until we discover their remains, we will most likely be held in the horizontal plane of repetition.

When a person dies in shock or violence, inflicted by the self or others, a part of the spirit becomes entrapped in the lower astral dimension, within the astral web surrounding the place of death. The disenfranchised spirit might also affix itself somewhere the personality deemed safe, such as a childhood place of play or condolence. As that negative energy is crystallized, it becomes an open invitation for like energies to feed upon, both in the astral and from other interdimensional spaces.

Vows and contracts are the threads that hold the spirit in the web of unresolved themes. We cannot find new relationships or expressions of the self because we are treading the waters of our emotional conclusions of the past. Think carefully when you hear yourself utter a vow or make a contract that has an emotional element to it. "I'll get even with you," or "I'll never trust again," may come back to haunt the shadows of that from which you now wish to be free. What you speak or think is charged with enough energy to carry it into manifestation.

After a person has released a difficult or negative lifetime, I must inquire, "Ask your Higher Self if any part of your spirit is caught there." Finding it to be true, I feel a great joy to witness the freeing of such a fragment of a whole, knowing that this person will now have a sense of being totally present, perhaps for the first time in this lifetime. It is a great relief to recover the part of the spirit that is entrapped and release it back into the cosmos. It is instantly transmuted into pure energy, from which we can build anew the spirit of our human heart.

Unencumbered by such sorrow, the spirit soars to new heights from which it can reclaim its magnificence. In a burst of all remembrance and relativity, a new depth of the eternal now can be experienced that will awaken humanity from the slumber of past and future myths.

We have become convinced that life itself is a linear thread composed of yesterday, today, and tomorrow. It is not. All of the content of the past is with us as energy. It might be a residue or remembrance, a thoughtform, or even an object filled with nostalgia. Today seems like an interminable holding tank for tomorrow, which is already in the mold of our unconscious restrictions.

Most of us become lost in the linearity of the third dimension. We suffer the illusion that we can only think or do one thing at a time. Linear reality is merely an old habit of the defensive mind. Since we anticipate that our actions and ideas will be challenged, we defend them in the most rational, deductive way we can. This is the cause of much confusion because in this singular mode, we simply cannot view all the pieces of the puzzle. We pretend one reality, one dimension, and defy the meaning of the stars above us and the Earth beneath. Like Don Quixote and his windmills, we are entrapped in an incessant response to the sound of our own voice swirling in the wind. We think ourselves alone.

SPIRIT BORROWING

Our tie with the astral dimension is more than just spirits left there. Whole worlds of beings live within the many different strata of the astral. Most important to humans are the kingdoms of nature. It is not just their bodies, but their spirits that play an important role in human potential and reality.

The shamans from every culture and corner of our Earth have ventured into relationship with the spirits of animals and rocks, to learn the secrets they hold. They are the shape-shifters who can move into the body of an ally and utilize its form to create some effect, or to cause a change that will then ripple out through the edges of astral strata and seep into other dimensions. This occurs because they have opened the astral sleeve that interfaces separate realities.

The shaman engages in a kind of "spirit borrowing" that allows him or her to take on the spirit of another being. This is a process of great skill and mastery concerning the ability to move between the dimensions safely without becoming "possessed."

American Indians would speak about honoring the spirit of the animal or plant one eats; to take in the body is to take in the spirit, as well. If the borrowing is done with care, the spirit will lend its wisdom and power to the one seeking its gift. By the same token, we might "borrow" the spirit of an animal that becomes our totem or which represents the qualities we exhibit or seek. We take on its attributes and in exchange, it is protected by our commitment to its spirit. This is a symbiotic system which ensures that the balance of nature is kept.

These profound teachings urgently need to be passed on to future generations. How can we teach our children to hold nature sacred when, especially those growing up in cities, might never chance upon an animal in the wild throughout their entire childhood? We can borrow from the Native Americans the practice of selecting an animal whose attributes or personality match that of the child, and help him or her to identify with that animal, learning everything about it, especially its spirit. We can call this imagination in school curriculums, but the result will be that children learn how to feel deeply into the unseen worlds to find meaning in life. As they commune with the spirit of another, they will embrace their own spirit — something that most adults have never touched — and Mother Nature will once again take up her sacred role of teacher to humanity. It is time to ask the Native Americans and

Treading Lives == 103

others, who have practiced these skills for generations, to teach them to us all.

In the past, one's singular animal spirit was a primary relationship for an entire lifetime. Now, the winds of karmic transformation have quickened so much that it might behoove us to change our focus throughout life's stages, so as to access more than one animal spirit. By the same token, you might feel many different animals calling to you to make the connection.

Many people today attempt to practice "spirit borrowing" through drugs or playing at shamanistic practices and rituals. While the lessons to be learned there are profound, the re-entry into these realms needs to come from a different place. We have all been shamans before, and our lack of self-identity in today's world causes us to seek desperately for something through which we can identify ourselves. The magnet for this magical learning comes from treading lives, in which these experiences are one's own memories from a time when it was much easier to know the self through stylized ways of living, such as the shamanistic role in a society. Indeed, the shaman's heart should belong to everyone, that we might feel the life in all worlds and bring it into harmonic helpfulness in our own.

Treading lives that teach us about "the Spirit that moves in all things" brings a new sense of belonging into our present life's experiences. Not only have we all lived lifetimes in which we connected to the spirit of nature, but some of those lifetimes are going on now, simultaneously!

When our reality includes spin points into other dimensions, those aspects relating to the other worlds tend to continue their existence even after the third-dimensional body has dissolved; spiritual and emotional experiences become genetic seed. This is why they can be readily viewed in the spiritual DNA by those who have developed clairvoyance. The coordinates within the Soul's matrix that correspond to overlapping themes can be activated when the consciousness rests on any point within the hologram that is associated with them. Those lifetimes resonating with our present themes work in concert to expand our awareness.

Almost never do we experience simultaneous lifetimes on the same plane. There may be thousands of Soul friends across the planet who are from your Soul group and very close in frequency; you will hold your Soul spark in only one body. You may be able to project that spark through your astral body into other dimensions or even to other places on the planet, but those who attempt to actually enter other bodies are creating karma through possessive intent.

Though there is a thin line between astral delusion and simultaneous reality, if we reach to our Divine Source we can accommodate the experience of being a part of only one infinite and loving Soul, that holds all form and expression within its embrace.

If perchance we might find a moment of silence, we could slide along its slippery smooth corridors until we come upon the center of our being. From this point of illumination, we can look out at our creations: many bodies, many lives. We might begin by accessing the angelic kingdom at the top of the astral spheres. From this illuminated space, we could link up the heavens and the Earth. By treading ever so lightly, we could open the seam into the higher dimensions and the beings who await our company.

When the Soul selects a "pivotal" lifetime with the intention of accelerated growth, the Soul Body becomes a beacon for other Soul friends to progress in their growth as well. Thus it is that many Soul particles may piggyback through one physical body into our karmic realities. They are treading lives by bridging the dimensions in order to amplify their Soul lessons. So it was with Buddha and Christ and many others who have come to reset the human seed. Through their enlightened frequencies, those in body and those sleeping within the universal womb have been given the resources to create new worlds.

SOUL GROUPS

Soul essence knows no boundaries. It does not isolate itself in the folds of inside and outside, of that which is not and that which is. It flows in the currents of the cosmos and ignites all other substances with its properties. It has no beginning and no end. There is nothing separate from it. The Soul essence is of infinite age, size, and shape, eternally pulsing outward toward new universes. Between the pulses, it rests in the sigh of creation, the ultimate power of birthing. We are its child. We are a part of its all-embracing oneness.

Within its wholeness, the Soul essence allows the natural current of its flow to manifest seemingly different forces on the plane of existence. That is why we feel ourselves to be so unlike one another. Perhaps you are a waterfall or a sea, a still pond or a raging river. You will relate to the other essence droplets of your own kind and may never know that the sea becomes the rain that becomes the river which flows home to the sea.

Though the Soul essence clothes itself in individual bodies, it never loses the integrity of the universal web. The connecting links cannot be cut because the core thread is beyond the substance of matter.

This truth holds two very important aspects for human awareness; the first is that of embodiment. The Soul essence carries its spark into embodiment and when its purpose is completed, it lifts out of the body and disseminates its spark to reverberate throughout the ethers. In the death process, people exclaim, "I am a trillion particles of light!" Each cell of the body contains the story of the carbon atom, told throughout the entire universe. This means that we never lose anyone. As they are freed from physical boundaries, their Soul essence calls ours upward to sense the threshold, the veil between the manifest and the unmanifest. This is how we learn and remember about our spiritual Source.

The second aspect is that we can gather and harvest the greatness of all beings who have ever touched human form. Their breath and their consciousness travel in the etheric flow, and thus influences our own beingness. Time and space have no effect on Soul essence. When one learns a great lesson or has a revelation, it echoes out and is carried onward by all the other sparks, whether or not they are in body. We must practice the expansion of our consciousness to become aware of these supporting energies, so that we do not fall into the pitfall of separation at this propitious moment in our evolution. There is great wisdom and help all around us if we reach out for it.

The third millennium holds a promise of great joy and peace. It will not happen around us or to us; we must manifest it ourselves. We are a collective Soul group who are having an initiation about universal potential. We are here to create a new species of humans who are fully conscious and can manifest all that connects us to the higher energies of ecstasy and bliss. Our new species will be able to go beyond the wants and needs of the individual and into a golden era of spiritual advancement that will completely change the way we live our lives.

The hologram of existence begins and ends in the spirit, and it is this spiritual connection that can be used in all its potential to change our reality. To sit in meditation or prayer is the most powerful way to embrace our Soul's heritage. To meditate with others is a most powerful affirmation of our oneness. Beyond the thoughts of doubt, the fears of emotion, there is a place of communion where our converging energies can be focused on something more important than our personal lives; they can be focused in the Divine Source, within our existence.

The challenge is not to deny our personal world and all the opportunities it provides us for growth, but to integrate ourselves into a greater whole. What we manifest, as a part of that whole, becomes what describes who we are!

SOUL FRIENDS

Certainly, the overriding karma we have with each other prevents us from even glimpsing the possibility of oneness. Without true spiritual comprehension, we do not yet recognize that everyone around us and, in fact, everyone on this planet is a part of the purpose of our reality.

Everyone you know is actually a Soul friend. Even people you don't know are Soul friends. "Enemies" too, are Soul friends. The ones you most despise are the ones you have chosen for your hardest lessons. You do not choose lightly. Only the ones you can trust to carry out a most difficult task will be considered your closest colleagues.

One of my favorite exercises is to meditate on the Higher Self of someone who is considered a negative person or an "honorable opponent." When you hold the vision of their Soul spark, which is the Higher Self, you cannot give power to the illusion that they are bad. If, as you perceive the energy of their Higher Self, you also ask your Higher Self to take form, your Emotional Body will be swept up into the frequencies of light, which are beyond comparison and reproach. If you like, you can allow the two Higher Selves to exchange gifts or merge.

I learned this technique when I worked in the National Men's Penitentiary in Bolivia. I had to find a way to see beyond the killer, the rapist, the cheat. I discovered that when you perceive the Divine aspect of someone who commits heinous acts or who hurts you, you must find new answers to the cycle of good and evil.

There is a place beyond these human concepts where the all-knowing, all-loving Soul resides. The old explanations of why we deserve punishment cannot carry us up to new spiritual octaves, where the laws of karma teach us to take responsibility for ourselves instead of waiting for an angry God to send someone to hurt us.

We know that we must make a transition, but we are afraid of being alone. We think that if we change anything, we will lose everything we have. Everyone is desperately seeking the safety of belonging to something or someone, to find some sense of power that we do not feel separately. Part of this longing is the cosmic plan to return us to oneness.

SOUL GROUPS

Who is your Soul group and how can you find them?

We here on Earth are all one Soul group. Though we may appear to be totally different, we hold the same essence. That essence expresses itself in many variations of the same cosmic theme. In human terms, the collectivity of Soul intention is intrinsically expressed in cultural and societal groupings, which organize microcosmic sub-themes into more universal avenues. Larger groups always allow a broad sweep of experiential history to define their specific evolutionary themes. This is true for whole races and cultures of people. Commonly held thoughtforms mold their way into life patterns which describe the limits of action and choice.

There are almost infinite categories of subgroups, which cross-reference each other to give us the maximum opportunity for growth. While in the past belonging to one major group was enough, today it is essential to relate to various groups because our lives have become so complex, in terms of our expanded world.

Each grouping activates a different facet of your being and helps you to realize the subtle interconnections that are possible in all groupings. In some, you might be the leader; in others, the student. As you learn to experience yourself within the opportunities of the group structure, you are simultaneously moving along the path of dharma and participating in a constant reshaping of the group, through your presence as well as your actions.

Though, as an individual person, you might seem the antithesis of a group's theme, there would be a perfect intersection between your own theme and that of your chosen group. Sometimes you learn as much from your opposites as you do from your mirror. You might choose a society, family, or mate that opposes you, in order to learn the lessons they present, whether the teaching in those lessons is to become more like them, to separate from them, or to find a way of being in peace with them.

We are all afraid to merge with groups. We have certainly had enough negative experience in collective bondage in this life, as well as in other lifetimes. The unfinished alliances from past civilizations are calling us to complete the karmic lessons we began together and find new creative solutions to our dilemmas. Ultimately, it may have more to do with how our consciousness communes, rather than any other kind of togetherness. Since we view life from a third-dimensional perspective, we think of a group as something physical. It may be the "Soul group" that reflects our ultimate truth. We will have to find a way to communicate with each other as Souls.

The channel of the Soul is outside of time and space. The line is never busy and although the person or group may not be conscious of the communication, they will receive it and respond within the ethers. These fabulous attributes of the spirit, which include telepathy and clairvoyance, are the birthright of all human beings.

I will never forget my experiences with telepathy in Russia. A people who had been suppressed for so long developed telepathic communication almost to an art. Though the content of their silent conversation was not always divine, there was a profound well-wishing attached to a quiet greeting. Even in the subway halls, there was a constant passing back and forth of information without more than a glance of the eyes. Yes, they knew each other, if only through the commonality of their life circumstances.

SOUL FAMILIES

We do have Soul families. Around the planet at this time, people from everywhere are meeting their Soul families; they are being attracted to each other without really understanding why. They just know that it feels good to be together. It might be a grouping around a central theme of politics, jobs, right living, ecology and environment, spiritual practice, self-help, or even sports and recreation. We are meeting each other in unusual circumstances and finding deep connections. In the past two decades, we have suffered a great confusion by which we interpreted that those deep recognitions must be about sexual merging, since that is a place that everyone feels the self. Instead, the closeness was really about Soul family and a kind of Soul connection we had forgotten, but which encompasses all the channels of relation.

We have a "lineage" given to us from interconnecting links around the hologram of our Soul family. It is composed of intrinsic qualities and attributes waiting to present themselves through the catalyst of our consciousness. All of the human strands of DNA represent our lineage. The DNA is itself multi-dimensional, in that the emotional DNA and spiritual DNA both piggyback onto the physical strands, and are very prominent in terms of the focus of that lineage. Beyond these, we may have creative, galactic, or spiritual lineages. Lineage is not linear; it flows in the hologram. It attracts to us like vibrations in others, which allow us to hook up through those powerful attributes we share. It is not something which separates us, but rather it moves inside us and supports our oneness.

Though on one level, we know that our cultures and individual blood families must be within our Soul group, we may feel closer to a stepparent or stepchild than to our own blood relatives. We may even feel more connected to our friends than we do to our family. Another culture or race may open our hearts more than our own. All of these liaisons need not cause us to feel separate or confused. We must realize that they are all part of our Soul family and have different roles to play in our lives. Actually, our primary "family unit" is with our Higher Self, though we may only perceive "family" to begin with ourselves and a mate.

Most of us seek an individual partner as our Soulmate, with whom we can reach some better or higher expression of ourselves. The person who ignites such a fire in our passion is usually a part of our karmic story. Because of our profound response to them, we ignore the indications that would show us their purpose as teachers in our lives. This often plays itself out in the old addiction of learning from the negative, with the result that we do not spend our lives with these "Soul" mates.

My Higher Self says that, for each person, there are 5,000 Souls on the planet that carry a vibration which could be considered that of a Soulmate! It is important to decipher the vibration, rather than project onto a person. Much of that projection has to do with wanting what we perceive we lack and they have. Sometimes their physical appearance triggers unconscious memories of bodies we carried in other cultures or civilizations. We may be of a different facial category and yet want to make a romantic connection with them because of karmic contracts. This is important because the shape of the face, (round or rectangular, for example) describes the cadence of each person's individual pulse.

We all know how it feels when we match our rhythm with another. Especially in terms of lovemaking, the more dissimilar the face, the less synergistic is likely to be the pulse frequency. Two people with widely divergent facial structures have a great deal to teach each other, but they will probably not be a close match sexually. It is interesting to note that after people have lived many years together, their facial features tend to become more similar.

After the sexual division which took place in Atlantis, we truly became fixated on using sexual expression as the way to come back into oneness and lessen the pain of separation. Perhaps because of the Atlantean genetic experimentation, we focused on the physical aspects of union and locked ourselves into the pattern of penetration in order to be sure there was a connection between two bodies. As far as we know, there is no other group besides the animals of Earth that use penetration as a form of mating or communion. The galactics, angels, and virtually all others do not use sexual penetration as part of their merging or procreative dance. Without the locking of two physical bodies, they may be able to merge in a deeper way. We try to attain an emotional bond by having penetrated each other, while they seem to pass right through one another, allowing a completion and continuing of the flow, rather than being stuck in the channel. As we move more into androgyny, perhaps we will be able to refine our experiences of merging so that we touch the Soul, as well as the body.

INTERSPECIES COMMUNICATION

Speak life, speak well

There are other Soul groups that are important to us that we never consider because of our limited concept of the Soul. We feel that the unique human capacity to remember and cognate is a part of what it is to have Soul. Since other species do not seem to have these characteristics, we pronounce them Soulless. Nothing could be further from the truth. For example, though animals reside mostly within the realm of instinctual realities, they have the capacity to enter into relationship with those who have developed intuitive expression, much the same way that our intuitive communication is activated by the presence of more advanced beings.

It is not uncommon for people and animals to have telepathic communication. Certainly, many people have reported that their beloved pets have been born anew in other bodies to continue their relationship. People sometimes identify pets they have now, in other lifetimes. We could perhaps conclude that this is just the result of emotional need, but even the slightest possibility of it is intriguing enough to ask what it could mean to us. The connection between ourselves and the animal kingdom is far more profound than we realize.

The major block to interspecies communication is our misunderstanding about intelligence and its application to manifestation. We have created a world in which our buildings, books, and concepts are the signature of our success in adaptability and control over the environment. I can't help but engage in a bit of whimsical fantasy as I contemplate the whales peacefully sounding to each other all history, current information in the minutest detail, and intimate social, familial relationships regardless of distances, while we struggle with our televisions and computers to comprehend what is going on by trying to translate each other's languages and cultures.

The reality of whales is totally fluid. Perhaps they have internal, multi-dimensional worlds that supply their awareness with everything they want or need. I have sat in dinghies in the quiet lagoons of Baja California while mother whales came alongside, ever so gently. They raised themselves up on top of the water, for me to touch their backs as we each looked into the eye of the other.

That probing, totally conscious stare was not one of idle curiosity, but a look of great knowing and intention.

Why do we humans think we have so much more than others? Do the whales, who have inhabited this planet for so much longer than we, have nothing to show for their millions of years of existence? Perhaps they have gone beyond external dependence. What a wondrous thing it would be to know their minds! We pride our greatness on what we have built to control our surroundings, while other species have adapted themselves to the environment. If adaptability were the measure of intelligence, many other species would outdistance us. Even the loathsome virus can recreate itself to find a place in a changing world. What would we learn from a virus if we could communicate directly with its reality? Such organisms are the masters of versatility, a most desirable feature in today's world. In our third-dimensional world, we certainly seem to be teetering precariously at the top, but as we begin to discover other-dimensional realities, we may find ourselves contending with a completely different perspective of values.

We have made a grave error to think that intelligence has to do with quantity or size descriptors, such as brain size. Could we measure the weight of a virus' intelligence? To search only among similar species with large brains for signs of awareness is to reflect our own disconnection with the intelligent forces around us. To presume that a central brain is the best and highest of nature's designs might be rather limited in scope.

Our difficulty comes from the conclusion that life travels on a trajectory from one point to another. Consciousness can be sonic, synergistic. When we make the leap to the holographic brain, we may discover whole new universes of which we never dreamed!

Both the animal and plant kingdoms are vibrant with intelligence and spiritual essence. Not only do they nourish, protect, help, heal, and comfort us, but they put forth great energy to guide and inform us in ways that could make the difference in our survival.

Up until now, our ignorance has caused us to misunderstand them and completely miss their message.

Many of us are now having experiences of special communications with animals and plants, as they are trying to help us return from our isolation. Let me share with you just two of the messages I have received from the animal and plant kingdoms that have been important to me:

The first one came from the birds. I was lying in the sun at my father's house in Sedona, Arizona. My consciousness was drifting lazily from thought to thought as I simultaneously enjoyed the smells of the high desert and the energy of the magnificent red rocks that I feel are so nourishing to my heart.

Suddenly there was a cessation of motion which I have experienced on several other propitious occasions. One rarely notices the sounds or flutter of insects, since their kinetic energy is too fast for our awareness. However, when the incessant motion stills, even for a second, there is an alarm that sounds in the instinctual body, saying that something unusual is happening. The birds stopped all their singing and movement and I became acutely aware of their silence. Within that same lull, I received an imprint from the birds that there had been a terrific shock in the atmosphere. The winds and the air itself had been blasted by some incongruous energy that had made itself felt around the globe. I instantly knew that it was about radiation, although I could not comprehend how or what. Later, I was to learn of the accident at Chernobyl, Russia, which was the source of the atmospheric shock.

I could not describe exactly how the birds had transmitted the information to me. It was about molecules, currents, and light. Perhaps some aspect of bird existence (which is within the primordial heritage of human evolutionary energies) opened a bridge within me to those specific sensibilities of the birds. I could only say that it was relayed to me and I understood it from some ancient "bird part" of myself that I cannot explain. Yet, the information was precisely correct. It has created a bond between myself and the birds. I notice that I am very aware of them and watch the birds in a new way. They seem to be more plentiful in my life now.

The other incident is about a message from the plant kingdom that I feel is very pertinent to this planetary moment.

I had just written an introduction to a charming book, *Das Geheimnis der Sonnenblume,* by Trutz Hardo. It is a sweetly illustrated story about a young boy who ventures into the garden of an old man, who teaches him to hear the humming of the flowers and what each is saying. The sunflower is the closest to us because of her tall countenance and her symmetrical beauty.

After I finished writing about the importance of tuning in to the sunflower, I returned to my car to find the tantalizing surprise of a giant sunflower. It had been placed there by one of my cranial healers, Carlo Castiglione, who knew nothing of the fact that I had just been writing about sunflowers.

The sunflower was so magnificent that it stirred a great sense of joy in me. Feeling a kind of absolute silliness and abandonment, I pressed the sunflower against my right ear as I bounced along the dirt road towards home. "Speak to me, speak to me," I challenged to my beautiful flower.

All of a sudden, I felt and heard a very clear humming in my ear. It was a strong, low hum in a masculine tenor. I felt as if I were transfixed by its vibration and I found myself holding my breath so as to not interfere with its energy coming into me.

The sunflower began to speak to me in a surprisingly serious manner. Its message included visual pictures of several small landscapes. One was of a rock with lichen on it, and a shaded area big enough to shelter about three people beneath it.

The sunflower spoke gently but firmly about the relationship between humans and nature. The thrust of its message was that people must understand that every place they stop in nature has spirit and is therefore sacred. We do not need to go only to those places we call "power spots" to receive the gift or exchange with the energies. Anywhere we chose to sit and focus, there are energies that will communicate with us and give us information we need to balance our world. There was a strong sense of concern for what humans are doing and the importance of asking the nature spirits to help us.

The effect of the sunflower's communication to me lingered for a long while. I felt as if I had been in the presence of a great teacher with a very powerful energy field. With a flash of realization, I remembered a thought I had been working on about what kinds of activities I wanted to present in a weekend workshop with people who would come to Galisteo to be with me. I had been wondering where to take them in the Galisteo area so that they could feel the wonderful energies from the sky and the land that are so important to our consciousness. The sunflower had answered my question.

How could the sunflower have accessed my thought frequencies? It had been cut and should have been dying. I felt the power of its will, and simultaneously, my commitment to pass on its message.

The earth and rock spirits of the mineral kingdom have sentient qualities that can inform humans of historic events beyond our present span of recognition. As a child, rocks always spoke to me. I kept it a secret until I was thirty years old and, after confiding it to a colleague, discovered that scientists have found rocks emit an electrical pulse, suggesting that even inert matter has a life force. Think of the power of gems, crystals, and other incredible gifts from the mineral kingdom in our lives.

We may not comprehend the fantastic possibilities offered us from the other kingdoms, but we must investigate them to gather any information that might instruct us about how to proceed into the invisible worlds around us. Interspecies communication could be a great tool in opening our future to a solar neighborhood that is calling upon us to participate. There are untold Soul groups in the universe, separated from us only by the thin veils of dimensional sleeves. As we develop new faculties to perceive them, we will embrace the wisdom of the devas, the angels, and the galactics, as they come to embrace our own.

GODS AND GALACTICS

There is something ominous about an unsolicited prediction. It seeps into the bottom of your consciousness and waits just beyond awareness, until its prophecy is potentiated by associated circumstances; then it rises up like a geyser you knew would burst forth and yet could not anticipate.

Somewhere inside, you must know that you are manifesting that prophecy because you always trust what someone else says more than you trust yourself. In some twisted form of politeness, you want them to be right, even at your own expense. If it is a negative one, the inner voice says, "I knew that would happen," and so throws its power behind the prediction. If it is a positive one, you hold so tightly to it that the sheer force of your focus brings it to fruition.

When a psychic told me not to travel alone because in three or four days I would have a contact with extraterrestrials, I was pleased and scared at the same time: pleased because I had been focusing on manifesting that contact, and scared because the reality of it held many unanswered questions.

I have always had a yes/no relationship with ETs. I have had various contacts with different groups, and though on the one hand I have often felt fantastic elation through their presence, on the other I have held a negative judgment or hesitation, based on my interpretation of their spirituality.

I wonder if our fascination with the galactics is an interim step, taking us out of a bad relationship with religion, until we can find a new body for our own Divine Source. I have to laugh at the absurdity and tenacity of our old thoughtforms that God and the Divine can only be expressed in human terms. Anything else could not be described as holy without the risk of sacrilege. I have much disdain for this colloquial point of view in my intellectual mind, yet there it was, hiding in some subterranean sludge of ancestral inheritance!

We humans insist that the gods must have private and emotional relationship with us. We have not learned that the essence of All that Lives is a sacredness in and of itself.

Despite my reservations, I had a re-occurring vision for many years, in which the best of our scientists, scholars, and leaders could come together with other species from across the galaxy, to share information and embrace each others' unique realities. In the past, I thought what was needed was a special physical place for our encounters, protected from the outside world and built to accommodate various environmental requirements. I knew that humans would have to quicken their energy so that they could withstand the heightened states of radioactive environments and other energetic anomalies that are natural to some extraterrestrials.

Now I know that rather than a place, what is necessary is a *state of mind* that allows human consciousness to incorporate and integrate the signals of the multilevel information that are a part of such meetings. The "others" too, are in great need of refining their style of communication with us.

Over the years of varied contact with different galactic presences, I have developed a sense of humor concerning both our

clumsiness and theirs, in terms of attempting to include and sometimes intrude in the realities of each. This canyon interlude is a
great example of debunking the breathless hope that anyone from
another dimension might be of the highest wisdom or a true rep-
resentative of Divine Source:

THE FLAG

I started out with my seventeen-year-old son, David, for a two-
day stopover in a magical canyon that I had discovered some time
before, while looking for suitable sights to establish a permanent
base for human/ET rendezvous.

David and I chose a beautiful spot, a short distance from an
emerald green pool that flowed down in a narrow stream under a
massive 100 ft. cliff. Because of the narrow width of the small canyon at that point, we literally slept with our feet at the water's edge,
facing the blank screen of that high canyon wall. We used no tents
and the stars were so magnificent in their intensity, it was hard to
forego their magnificent stimulation and sleep.

My body is an incredible pulsar of sensitivity to energetic environments. I always feel earthquakes and volcanic eruptions before
they occur. It is a sense of vague pressure in my solar plexus, accompanied by a kind of sloshing feeling which makes me irritable and
heavy at the same time. Since the energy of any natural event pre-
cedes it, it is easy to perceive the buildup to critical mass that then
explodes into manifested action. I have learned to ask my body if
these disruptive sensations belong to me, so that I do not confuse
my own internal energies with those of the planet.

I slept restlessly, hoping and waiting for the night to bring me
this mysterious encounter. We always think anything uncontrollable and powerful belongs to the night, and this time it was true.
Deep in the night, I was awakened by a very rough sensation of
something shaking my brain. When I was awake enough to clearly

perceive it, I felt as if something had intruded into my brain and was attempting to override it with a very clumsy kind of energy that did not feel as if it fit my brain pulses.

I opened my eyes to an astounding sight: a white screen, placed over the cliff wall as if a projector had been turned on and had lighted up the entire face of the wall. Then, the most shocking thing occurred. Through my brainwaves, through my brain itself, certain images seemed to be projected upon the wall that were an almost outlandish attempt at speaking "human." The ETs were attempting to communicate symbolically to me. There was a rainbow and a pot of gold, an American flag, as well as several other symbols that I subsequently forgot. It was as if they had been reading children's stories or only had a limited visual vocabulary. I felt immediately annoyed by their choices, none of which seemed relevant to me personally.

The American flag stuck in my head as totally incongruous and in opposition to my own feelings. Since living abroad, I had come to feel politically that a flag only accentuates the separation between countries. I felt that we should at least have a world flag to acknowledge ourselves as one global family. The image of the American flag made me aware that they were attempting to relate through a stereotypical base of symbols. It was a sensation of being co-opted into someone else's impersonal reality that disallowed my individual preferences. I loathed it!

I have no idea how long the images were projected, for as soon as my mind began to fight the image of the flag as a limited expression of who I am, it was gone. All that remained was a rather disrupted feeling in my brain, as if some divisive force had failed in coming into sync with it. At that point I realized that the extraterrestrial groups would have to be reviewed in terms of compatibility with humans, and not be accepted only because they could somehow beam themselves into our earthly environment.

The next day I felt exceptionally irritable and tired. David had not awakened and was somewhat incredulous of my story.

Everyone feels the discomfort of finding themselves attempting to describe some reality in which others do not share. The loneliness of individual reality is a painful burden to us all. In the bright light of the morning sun, I sat facing that wall in great dismay and disappointment. These were not the ETs who would work with us to alleviate the difficulties we face on our Planet Earth!

It was then that I began to ponder how they could have been so clumsy, so inept at comprehending the human psyche. All of the portrayals of ETs or galactics as being completely nonhuman, devoid of emotions and mechanical in thought patterns, caused me to contemplate the convergence of technological mastery and Soul essence. I realized that there are many species and even races of galactics, and we would have to learn how to call to us those who were more aligned to our frequencies.

I had to wrestle again with the understanding that all which exists is a part of the Divine Source, even if it does not coincide with our human point of view. It is hard to feel the Soul of a creature that has no emotional content or who may even be a clone, created by some technological process. Since that time, I have been able to resolve the dichotomy by comprehending that the Soul of the creator rests in all creation. The clone carries the karma and frequency of those who create it. Some humans have trouble acknowledging Souls of animals, which in comparison to these galactic bodies, seem practically the same as ourselves!

Indeed, the concept that similarity of body equates to similarity of essence is very misleading. It seems that our human Emotional Body acts as a barrier between ourselves and others, whereas communicating with different species frees us from the constraints of suppositions as to who we are that introduce so much negativity and judgment.

It is important for us to trust our feelings in regards to other beings, rather than what we presume to be true from what we see. Certainly, when it comes to ETs, neither our fears nor our fantasies are very good indicators.

FRIENDS

I once had an experience with some space beings that was a magnificent teaching about the irrelevance of form. I was living in Bolivia in a place called the Valley of the Moon. My bedroom was on the second floor. It had a big window through which I could gaze upon the stars, which seemed so close (at 13,000 ft.) that I could almost touch them.

During one season, I was awakened three nights in a row by a strong sense of presence, as if a star were actually entering my room. It was exactly two o'clock. I could see the constellation of Orion through the window, and — a little further away — a bright star which held my gaze. The first two nights I just lay there in the energy until it would abruptly disappear and I would fall back to sleep.

On the third night, as I was awakened, I felt a tremendous magnetic pull, which lifted me from my room and out into the cosmos. There I encountered a small group of amorphous beings who had a shape like Casper the Ghost, with one large eye centered in the upper portion of the body. They were nothing like the fabled Cyclops of Greek mythology, and I felt utterly safe and protected by their presence. They were definitely friends.

They communicated with me through feeling sensations and I remember little direct conversation, except that they conveyed to me that they were from the star Sirius, which was the bright sparkling one I had seen through my window.

They performed a series of experiments with me, which I experienced as a sensation of being thrown up into space — higher and higher — and then being caught by them. It was done very gently and with a wondrous feeling of all-embracing love. I felt a bit badly when, at last, I had to communicate to them that I was sure I would disintegrate if they threw me up any higher into space. It was a kind of fizzing sensation that took over my body, and I experienced a molecular expansion, as if I was spreading out into the cosmos.

They immediately stopped moving my body, and I had a very distinct impression of their concern for my welfare. I found myself back in bed, wide awake and feeling as if the entire sky were inside my body. The next day, I was walking down the main avenue of La Paz when I happened to glance at the display in the window of a bookstore. I noticed a small book with the title, *The Aliens Amongst Us* — such an intriguing title that I had to stop and see what it was about. I was disappointed to discover that I could not browse through it, as it was wrapped in cellophane. Reluctantly, I bought the book and opened it in a secluded corner, where no one would see me with such outlandish material.

To my great shock, I opened the book to a full-page drawing of the very beings I had encountered the night before! The text described them as a large grouping of several hundred sandstone statues with one eye, which stand somewhere in the desert of central Africa. I knew then that I must seek them out someday and find out who has been in contact with them and what they came to teach us. All I can carry away from that encounter is that whoever they are, despite their strange bodies, they are my friends.

On another occasion — in fact the last occasion in which I had direct contact — I was given an entirely different experience, but one which also caused me to contemplate human perception of good and evil.

I was asleep in my bed. Somewhere in the middle of the night, I felt a probe into my brain faculties. It was an entirely different quality of probe from the one in the canyon. Ever so gently, it called me forth from my sleeping, dreaming state. It did not have a quality of seduction. It had a very clear resonance that seemed to merge with my brain patterns. As I was lifted from sleep, I experienced a telepathic message which said,

"Wake up! We are here."

As I awoke, I turned my head and there at the end of my bed were three galactic beings. They were quite small, about three feet tall, with a beautiful whitish body, large head, and large oval eyes.

They seemed to be sending me energies of complete compassion and peace.

Instead of trusting those vibrations, my mind interfered and I thought of the picture on the front of a popularized book describing human abduction. The picture showed the very same characteristics. In spite of my feelings of friendship and sense of non-interference from these gentle beings, I crossly demanded that they go away, sending them a kind of thought form which said, "You are not the good guys! Get out!"

They instantly moved back from the bed and disappeared.

Then something very shocking occurred. As I lay in bed, contemplating what had happened, I felt the voice of my own Higher Self clearly speak to me. It conveyed something I shall never forget.

"These beings were here as an opportunity for you to give something to them."

I felt struck in the heart at the realization that they had simply wanted my help, that I had something to give them, and yet had not even allowed the possibility of finding out what. For years I had witnessed space ships. I had called forth to the galactics and now, only because of someone else's interpretation about what or who is bad, I had lost the very opportunity I had been waiting for. Furthermore, the base of this shallow decision had been the way they looked: that they had not been as "human" as others I have met!

We humans have so imprinted the concept of primordial survival, almost on the level of "eat or be eaten," that we lose the opportunity to be the givers, to recognize within ourselves the power to affect the destiny of others, rather than presume that outside forces will always control our destiny.

That interlude haunted me for many months and I would often call them back, but they never returned. It did serve as a great lesson to me to wait long enough until the purpose is clear before making rash decisions.

One day as I was working in my study, I glanced at the shelf where I keep gifts people give me. I saw a small sculpted head of a being with exactly those same features, which my own daughter, Megan, had given me when she was about eleven. As I thought about the gentleness and wisdom I felt coming from those small bodies, I reflected on how we change completely from one incarnation to another, but there is always an interconnecting link available to us, if we wish to use it.

Those three beings that visited me had a oneness that felt to have come from the way their minds flowed as one, a gentleness that, if not humanoid, certainly was recognizable to me. It held away my fear and signaled to me a total freedom of response and choice throughout the brief encounter. No, they were not insisting upon a response; they were waiting for me to be the initiator of something that still ripples as a profound question in my heart, as well as my mind.

Throughout the ages, there have been many gods and deities worshipped by humans, most magical and divine. We have sought, and always will seek, to find our source — to comprehend how it is that we have been brought to life, that we do live, and for what ultimate purpose. There must surely be a Divine Force flowing through the cosmos that nurtures the existence of all life and we must acknowledge that there is a hand that consciously shapes life, experiments with species, and designs new and varied forms.

Why do we insist that the hand of God be a human hand? To be sure, we are only one expression of artistic endeavor. Just as we humans are reaching a point that we can manipulate genetic structure and therefore the form and kinds of species, it would only be intelligent to presume that this genetic art has gone on throughout the eons and will continue to go on, not only in our neighborhood but even from one universe to another.

Many of the great historical and religious doctrines relate that "the gods came down and seeded the daughters of man." Were not those interchanges for some great cosmic purpose? Did they evolutionize the human species?

Even at this moment, it is clear that we need another cosmic infusion to lift us out of a stale encapsulation that has isolated us from the eternal pulse. That is exactly what is happening now: we are being infused with a new kind of energy. Even without physical contact, this new energy will bring a new look into the eyes of our children and a new relationship with the cosmos.

It is possible, even probable, that several species want to claim humans as their own private experiment. They may need us to rebalance their spiritual and emotional genetic weak points. Our heart energy could be a missing link in the coordinates of many diverse species who have lost the feeling of their spiritual heritage.

The possibility that others may see us as a link to the God-force seems somewhat remote, if not totally ridiculous, since we are certainly only "raw" material at this point. The angels and others are much more enlightened than we, but we are the only ones carrying the seed in concrete physical form. Our spiritual heritage is rich and full of ecstatic potential that we have not yet realized ourselves. The others are perceiving something in us that we might pursue as well.

Up until the present, the practice of borrowing or extracting genetic material has been one of incredible abuse throughout the galaxy. No explanation or permission is deemed necessary, and we are horrified at the personal accounts of people who have experienced some form of extraction of genetic material at the hands of seemingly unscrupulous aliens.

Even more shocking are the results of information gathered from thousands of Light Institute sessions in which we have explored the theme of "Memories of Extraterrestriality." When asked to find the cause of abduction and clinical experimentation, almost 100% have discovered that they had actually volunteered to come into human form to supply the genetic material because the abductors were their own group. Perhaps it truly is an illusion that they are someone else. They are ourselves!

At The Light Institute we have come to distinguish between an abductee and a contactee as the difference in conscious awareness. The abductee has eclipsed any knowing of such relationships, and the contactee is simply aware of being a part of the larger scheme of things. Often, the person has either asked to have the memories erased or the galactics have chosen to cause amnesia in order to lessen the considerable strain of such awareness. At some point, the veil of memory may be pulled away to facilitate a more collective comprehension of what is happening on cosmic levels. Without this awareness, we will not be prepared for the coming acceleration.

This information has been a great shock and a tremendous relief to many people who have had these kinds of experiences. When they find themselves to be a part of something beyond this reality, they must expand their conscious recognition to include its purpose, or face the possibility of disintegration of the personality self.

Everyone, at one time or another, feels alienated or that they are not a part of this Earth. Have you ever felt that you did not come from your family? Many children make this kind of comment. We should learn to listen to these feelings, not just because they may be expressing an emotional state, but because it is entirely possible that certain genetic strains beyond our own may be moving through them.

Children often draw or speak about galactics in an attempt to express some relationship they feel towards them. They also commonly dream about space ships and visitations. It is very important not to shut them off from something that may be considered a fact of life in the future, just because you do not have firsthand experience of it at this moment. There are many new bits of information coming in to us, as the evidence of galactic reality mounts higher and higher.

One very common revelation within the extraterrestrial theme is the existence of a huge intergalactic station at which genetic material from around the universe is studied. People from all walks of life have seen and described this station in almost identical terms. Infinite, white laboratories receive genetic material and experiment on creations of new species which are then seeded into many different star systems. The station is not in our galaxy and is said to be larger than Planet Earth. What could this mean to our creation myths and our very tenets of existence?

As it was once necessary to see that the world is round, it is now necessary to see that we are a part of an inhabited universe and that we have an unprecedented opportunity to actually travel through it.

Viewing our own genetic advancements in terms of creating new hybrid plants and re-designing genetic strands in animals and even ourselves, it is not too farfetched to postulate that our species has been given new impetus through new genetic material over the millennia, to enhance our intelligence or to survive our environment here on Planet Earth. Since only God is the originator of the divine spark, neither these alterations or the theory of evolution is in opposition to the Divine. However, how these things occur is very much a concern, in terms of cosmic and spiritual ethics.

There have been many accounts of certain women becoming pregnant and carrying a fetus for a length of time, and then suddenly the entire pregnancy has disappeared. One such inexplicable occurrence happened to a female medical doctor who is well known, both professionally and as a spokesperson for the new science.

After a near-death experience, she felt that her psyche was opened into other-dimensional realms. She had an experience of abduction in which eggs were removed from her fallopian tubes. This occurred several times and after each time, she had vague memories of what took place and rather intense emotions of loss and depression When the truth came to light during sessions, she was able to work in a positive manner towards what she said was "… the ultimate inclusion of humans within a solar neighborhood."

Another woman had this very vivid experience:

"It was one of those warm summer nights when every cell within my body was humming and tingling with life and some strange antici-pation. The air was charged with the luminescence of a buttery full moon glow, as it rose like an all-encompassing blanket over the mountain top.

"We were spending a week on a friend's ranch and living in a wonderful teepee that embraced our bodies in its circular arms and breathed up into the heavens from the apex at the top, through which we could glimpse the stars.

"The night was magic and so were we, as we slowly, gently slipped into each other's bodies — past the language of fragrance, past the vulnerability of touch, through the unbounded passion and into the deepest pool of loving essence. Into the space of our oneness, suddenly came a presence — grand and intently focused.

"I opened my eyes into the face of a very large winged being with huge grayish colored wings. Why was he here at this sacred moment? An angel?

"No. There was something expansive but not glorious in his coun-tenance. 'What do you want?' my thoughts pleaded.

"His look informed me that he had achieved whatever it was and, as if the air rolled over in a wave motion, he was gone. It was only

moments before I knew that I was pregnant and wondered what this strange visitation would mean to the outcome of it. Immediately and throughout the next few weeks, my body exploded into all the symptoms of pregnancy. I was caught in the vast emotional sea of conflict and confusion about my life.

"Again, in a night of peace and intimacy, the winged being appeared and in a conversation of instantaneous communication and action, he informed me that his species had lost their capacity to reproduce and so were 'borrowing seed' from the humans. I felt no emotion come from him except a kind of quiet acceptance. I also knew that somehow he understood how hard this was for me.

"There was a sensation in my womb. I wouldn't say it was painful, just a kind of strange movement, and I knew that it was over. Indeed, the pregnancy symptoms disappeared as quickly as they had come, leaving me to wonder about the meaning of life and how we could ever know truth.

"Two years later I had a dream in which this child was brought to me. He had a strange energy field, almost human, but cast over by a serious demeanor very much like that of the winged being I had met. In his eyes was a look I shall never forget: a question. It was a question of feeling, a question of the heart."

I am fully convinced that if we are a cosmic experiment, we are having our own impact on those who come into our sphere of influence or carry our essence into their own life vessels. As we are mixed and recombined in the cosmic cauldron, our human essence is infiltrating all the other perpetrators of the evolutionary pulse.

The human heart has an as yet unfulfilled and unattained potential, a kind of power in its stretching that is felt out into the galaxy. Could it be that in all the genetic tinkering, the throbbing essence disintegrated, dried up, and that this heart quality could be looked upon as an available element of life? Perhaps its effect on variables in terms of individuals within a group might even be an essential part of natural evolution, rather than the "cookie cutter" genetic homogeneous perfection that is so much a part of our neighbors in the Galaxy. If we can accustom ourselves to this revelation, we can expect to find a new place in the universe, a new relationship to the Divine Force and to ourselves.

Faced with the presence of a new and strange group of beings, our predecessors could not make a distinction or a discernment about how to relate to them. They equated different skills of manipulating the environment as being indicative of magical and divine qualities. Literally every culture on the globe has held myths about the gods descending onto the planet in one form or another. Were these beings truly gods, or were they merely more advanced species of galactics, who gave great teachings and stimulus to human evolution and then left us to our own growth?

As I wander along the mesas of New Mexico, touching the petroglyphs of etched stars and beings with headdresses and belts around their waists, I cannot help but wonder about the story of their coming. Their remains in some parts of the world are truly awe inspiring. They focused the humans towards the heavens, and the steps rising up to the sky on the temples that worshipped them can leave no doubt that those who came into contact with them were convinced that they were, indeed, the gods.

Tragically, some of those conclusions led to the demise of peoples whose myths dovetailed into the appearance or actions of adventurers who were far from being gods. Such was the case of the Spaniards. As they arrived on the shores of the Americas with their superior weaponry and reflective armor, they fit the description of mythical stories in which the gods (who had come before and left such treasures of knowledge as astronomy, mathematics, and advanced healing techniques) would return from the direction of the east, clothed in the brilliant light of the cosmos. Thus it was that the galactics became the gods, and the adventurers from other lands masqueraded as the powers of the skies and brought destruction to the cultures they invaded.

There are many different species of galactics from infinite regions, even beyond our universe. To be sure, they come for some implicit purpose which we hope to be symbiotic. From some, I have felt no emotional body, no flicker of what we would term "conscience," that we would relate to our concepts of good or evil. From other cosmic species, I have felt a quality of compassion, some kind of expansive caressing that is detached, rather than the emotional kind of loving that we experience on our planes. There are those who come (as they did in ancient times) to bring us new potential, or to protect our Earth from our deadly explorations. One of my own experiences is an example of the incredible information they can pass to us:

For several months in my dreams and in some deep reservoir of my consciousness, I saw a space ship with a yellowish glow around its upper body. It had a kind of familiarity about it and I felt a sense of relationship, rather than the detached observations I had experienced with the many other ships I saw in the Galisteo area. On more than one occasion, I found that I would arrive someplace with a lapse of time and would have no awareness of how I got there. I felt that I was being taken frequently into this space ship without conscious awareness, and I often lay down in the hallway in front of the glass door, looking out over the Galisteo basin where the ships would come, clothed in their cloud cover.

One day as I was lying there in a dreamlike state, after watching a ship that had been sitting there for about two hours, I suddenly had a very alert awareness that I was again right up against the yellow portholes of the ship, as I had experienced before. This time, instead of the separated feeling of being on the outside of something impermeable, I somehow felt myself invited inside, without any sensation of resistance.

I knew that I was fully conscious in that theta frequency of very quiet stillness. There was a gentle adjustment to the environment, and then I recognized a group of four people standing around me inside the capsule. They looked surprisingly very much like me, and a tiny part of my mind touched a thought that they were manifesting their bodies that way to make me feel comfortable.

Within the circular shape of the ship was a computer with many lights, that reached almost completely around the circumference. They spoke telepathically to me, explaining about the information contained in the computer and its lights. It was apparently a computerized map of the Earth that conveyed what was occurring on global, political, cultural, and physical levels. None of that stayed in my mind, except one area that was illuminated in a way that attracted my attention. They told me that they had brought me into the ship to show me what was happening there. I had the awareness that it was somewhere in the Middle East.

What they told me made my blood run cold. They explained that because of ancient vendettas, children were killing children and that thousands of men, women, and children were being killed every day and were being buried in mass graves made of trenches. Furthermore, because of the hatred and vengeance, their astral bodies were putrefying in the lower astral dimension — so much so, that the Earth could not breathe. I was then given a visual perception of the astral bodies, which were causing a kind of polluted fog that was spreading out in every direction. They told me that I must tell as many people as possible about the situation, and show them how to release the dead from the astral dimension so that the Earth could again breathe the pure prana.

The technique was to visualize a large plane of white light, like a highway that is rising into the sky. We should encourage them to step up on the highway and return to those who loved them and were waiting for them. They telepathically showed me that some of those loved ones would be Souls they had traveled with in other lives, as well as this one.

When they had moved up along the pathway of light until they disappeared, we were to then draw the white light down through the top of our heads and into our stomachs and then to laser that light out in front of us. This would serve to clear our own auric fields of any residue from them.

After this teaching, I found myself back in my house, very awake and focused. There was no dreamlike quality to what I had just experienced, but rather an exceptional clarity of mind. I immediately made the video and audio tapes called "Death and Samadhi," which explained how to help spirits of the deceased to rise up out of the astral.

I saw no information in the news about this occurrence and began to feel a little unsure of what I had been shown. It was three months later that the news broke about mass graves uncovered in an internal war of hostility and vengeance amongst the people of Syria. The confirmation caused an intense jolt of reality, and I wondered if the galactics would ever return to converse with me again, and about what.

All of these profound experiences have caused me to feel a very real, if invisible, relationship to the cosmos. I have great compassion for those who find Earth a place of isolation. I know that it is imperative to access sky energies and bring them into our world, so that human embodiment is no longer in exile from home.

My Higher Self gave me a wonderful practice to help me anchor the sky. As if I were a child tasting the stars, it showed me to lick my index finger and hold it up to any star or constellation that attracts me. It usually feels like a cold spark of electricity striking my finger as energetic contact occurs. Then I touch my finger to the tip of my tongue as if I were sampling the most exquisite of elixirs. It creates a very minute trembling inside my body, a kind of far away ecstatic streaming. Through it, I know I am touching something that is a part of who I am.

It is inevitable that we come to embrace the fact that we are not alone, or even that we are not the ultimate species within our galaxy.

We are, indubitably, a tender race. Through our errors, we have come more than once to the edge of extinction, and have had to find expression of the wisdom so long lost with those who have come before us, even beyond our present historical certainty. If these beings from other planets have existed for unfathomable currents of time, what might they have learned about life itself, the secrets so incomprehensible to us, of cosmic law?

Deeply within my being, I know that neither law nor time stretches itself out in an infinite linear continuum. Rather, it arcs and curves and spins itself, infinitely re-gathering cause and effect, action and reaction, to reshape and recreate, and therefore through that pulse, moves forward. Then, I ponder, if these gods and galactics have had some hand in shaping our species, our past, and our future — if we intertwine, and curve together to create some kind of circling cosmic ripples of interconnecting consciousness — what is it then that we have to give to them? When I ask what could we possibly have that would draw them to us or this planet, I know that at least some part of the answer is held within the depths of the human heart.

Perhaps our sobs are being answered by a genetic matrix, which contains a recessive gene of feeling that longs to echo back to its source across the universe and throughout the cosmos!

FREE THE ANGELS

Sobbing is a language of its own. There are sobs of agony, of joy, and of ecstasy. There is the tiny whimpering of trepidation when you expect to be hurt. There are sobs of betrayal, of longing and regret. There is the great heaving sob when you are finished and have let something go. There are special sounds that accompany a trembling heart when you have come to a new discovery, and there is the absolute sigh of bliss when the gentle tears announce Divine presence.

In the healing room, we learn to distinguish each and all of these so that we know when to wait and when to speak when someone is sobbing. Sometimes even we are caught up in the energy of tears when someone connects to an aspect of their sacred essence. Beyond all the wrongs, the inertia, the judgment, there is a flicker through which one sees one's perfection. It might have been a gesture of true love, the clarity of wisdom, or a glimpse of the self wearing a celestial body such as that of an angel. The tears are the gentle touch of truth, confirming that which one would never dare to proclaim: to be a part of something perfect. It is almost more than we can bear. Yet, again and again it is shown to us in Light Institute sessions, and we who have the honor of witnessing these profound reunions may boldly insist upon seeing it not only in action, but at its very core, within the DNA structure of the genetic encoding.

The DNA viewing is what had precipitated the sobbing that was going on now. She was a woman in her late forties who had just re-lived an angelic experience and was viewing it on a strand of her DNA. There is something about the kind of confirmation one feels when one can see that sacredness is absolutely anchored into one's very core, something that creates an overwhelming response ... and the sobbing begins.

She described it as a gossamer seed of translucent pastel light which pulsed so sweetly that her whole body felt caressed in its love. She rose from the table a new being, one who trusted in her own goodness. She would not have to try to be angelic; it would come naturally to her without any thought or self-consciousness.

Angels always provoke a response of awe in us. So without malice, seemingly made of the purest light, they are perhaps the only beings we recognize as godly. Though we look very much like some races of angels, we can't fathom our connection to them. In truth, they are our cousin species, so close to us that we can dream of them, talk to them, and feel that they hover around us. We sing about them and even, once in a great while, may hear them in their celestial choirs. Artists have been instrumental in our awareness of angels by showing us their form and opening our hearts to their beautiful vibration. Artistic expression conveys the psychic, emotional, and spiritual energies that connect us to the angels.

One of my students, who experienced a lifetime as a famous artist, said that angels hovered around him each time he painted. Here is her comment:

"From the experience of one of my lifetimes as a famous artist, I discovered that I had three or four angels accompanying me while I was painting. I mainly worked on religious themes and my master-piece was a huge altar with the resurrection of Jesus the Christ. While

I painted, the angels told me how Jesus appeared physically. We had a big discussion about his nose. One day I decided to do a portrait of my little angelic friends. Since I couldn't see them, they told me what they looked like. Through the painting they became visible to others as well as myself."

(The description is one pertaining to the Cherubic race of angels.)

Though we in the western world tend to think of angels as heralds of the Judeo-Christian era, they have been depicted in almost all religions and cultures throughout time. Winged beings have been described for centuries in all parts of the world as a part of both mythology and culture. Within the angelic kingdom, there are many "races" such as the Seraphim, Cherubim, guardian angels, and archangels, to name a few. Each group has a characteristic body type and wing structure. On the other hand, there are many species of winged beings who look similar to angels but who are not. Gods and demons have worn wings to demonstrate their freedom from earthly laws.

Angels and humans have a long and varied relationship and our karma is closely linked with theirs. We have moved deeper into material form and taken up the yoke of free will, while they have lingered in the Light Body to remind us of our Source. Although to our eyes they appear to be eternal beings who have always been the same and always will be, their karmic relationship with us causes them to interface the timeless astral dimension with our world of change.

Within the astral dimension, there are many different statifications: from the deepest, darkest recesses of purgatory and hell to the highest octaves of the celestial heavens. The astral dimension is in simultaneous space with us, separated only by a veil through which our awareness rarely passes unless we are in a state of sleep or an altered state of consciousness. There, time does not exist as it does for us, and thus all the glories and the demons are transfixed in a dreamlike fog of endless continuity.

If we are to comprehend our universe and our place in it, we must see it as a dynamic and infinite pulse in which all of life continues to change and evolve. We have fostered thoughtforms insisting that nature is subject to evolutionary laws, but that the Divine and sacred are not. **All that exists evolves.** My Higher Self says, "God grows through you!" The God-Force is definitely experimenting with our infinite design, and we are also altering the Divine through our evolution. Sometimes it seems impenetrable to decipher who or what is overseeing this experiment, but as we undergo its reality, we will find that we ourselves are in some way the experimenters.

We were once much more like the androgynous form of the angels than we are today. After the sexual division experiment which took place in Atlantis, the male and female energies were separated. The human became more masculine in nature, even within the female body, and the gentle angelic realm was distanced while the Atlanteans created other beings, some of whom had wings. The yin angelic vibration was eclipsed by the Atlanteans' fervor for genetic manipulation. These acts of domination led to the desire for personal power and brought the world into the clutches of masculine laws of manifestation.

The angels have always been guided by their feminine qualities to work and live within a higher order that has not necessitated individual choice. Their consciousness is therefore easily held on very high frequencies, as the power of the whole maintains their light. Our light has been greatly diminished because we retreat from the blending of our energies and hold ourselves in the separation of the yang/masculine will. Our entire universe is now returning to the fluidity of the yin and this bodes well for the future of the humans, if we can internalize what the angels are showing us.

Though at this moment we may feel disheartened by the warring and negativity we are witnessing on the planet, these are only the dying cries of throwback genetic residues that will not continue in our genetic material. From this point onward, they serve no evolutionary purpose because of their destructive nature. We have reached an autonomous level in the experiment, in which our experience is illuminating the law of cause and effect so that our survival intelligence can realize the danger of this action to our species as a whole. As we bring forward the more enlightened strands of cosmic encoding, which offer us the awareness of our true purpose and potential, we will no longer seek survival by force, but rather embrace our creative adaptations. To this end, the angels are stepping forth, not to save us, but to help activate our own angelic genetics and qualities so that we can move into their frequency. Though they have much to teach us, we have a special role in their evolution as well. Ultimately, our knowledge of physical embodiment will be of great value in creating a new human species that can combine the subtle angelic frequencies with those of the physical planes. Our direct experience may be used to amplify their angelic genetic repertoire, passing back to them an element of physicality essential to their evolution!

Only recently has there been any discussion of the possibility that angels are real and can be accessed by "normal" people. Perhaps a century ago, you would have been burned for heresy had you claimed that you saw or talked to an angel. Today you might not only be listened to, but you might be praised. Our relationship with the angels is taking a new course, one that returns us to the powerful essence of the spiritual. The question is not, "Do they exist?" but "What shall we do with them?" How can we relate? We will want to cling to the angels because of all the celestial, galactic and devic species, they are the most human in countenance and the most admirable in action.

We have painted angels and prayed to angels for so long, and now we need them in all their glory, goodness, and possibilities, to illuminate this moment of transition so that we can see and feel goodness in our world. We do not believe it of ourselves, but we can believe it in them. It is necessary to complete the circle of relationship so that we internalize the angelic qualities and recognize them as an innate part of our angelic/human link. It is hard to imagine that such magnificent and powerful beings could be influenced by our decisions, and yet it is true that within cosmic law, all relationships are circular.

We must embrace the angelic species as our true teachers of human potential, while releasing them from the karmic indebtedness by which we have held them to be responsible for us and to protect us, simply because one of their species (Lucifer) was the focal point of cross-referencing with the human species through the exercise of free will. That single act of attempting to carry the light separately caused a sense of separation and dimming of conscious illumination that has lasted for eons. Who sat in judgment of that choice — the angels? If so, they created karma, which they are rectifying by helping us avoid such pitfalls. Since all experience gives a teaching, perhaps that is how they learned the laws of non-intervention and non-judgment. We must open our awareness of them as a species which is also in a process of evolution. It is certainly not now the angels' choice to sit in judgment of the humans. Good and evil is not their conversation; it is only ours. Fear of those two polarities was not introduced from above to below, it was plotted by humans through the projection of their own negativity, to reinforce their certainty that something bigger exists that would not accept human folly. How tragic it is that we cloak divine compassion and unconditional love in our rags of shame!

The relatively short term effect of the Luciferian attempt at illumination has led to an erroneous conclusion that the God-force wants to punish us for his impudent act of aggrandizement (by copying what God does), and that we therefore must stifle all possibility of being like God. These postulations can easily be revealed to be authored by human confusion, which cannot imagine that the Divine Force would want more and more resplendent light to enhance creation. It is almost ludicrous for us to project our illusions of ownership onto the Infinite, while all other evolutionary forces continually clone and copy and repeat successful qualities. Only the separated human would encumber the Divine Source with such pitiful motives while s/he still can only imagine "God" in human form.

Some people refer to humans as the "fallen angels" and discuss how Lucifer dared to use his free will to plunge us all, his heirs, into the pit of darkness. This has given rise to the almost universally held conclusion that we must struggle righteously to return to God's favor, while suffering to pay for Lucifer's "mistake." This is a myth perpetrated by those who feel humans should be relegated to realities of punishment and therefore control. It is so typically human to think that we inherit only the bad, but never the good. Our logic is one-sided and blame-oriented. If we inherited Lucifer's lust for free will, we also must have within us the magnificence of all angelic encoding, which he carried as well. Is it a seed awaiting its maturity, or are we the activation factor, necessitating only our decision to claim our own lighted inheritance? The conversation is not about him; it is about us!

Did Lucifer blaze free will into our genetic material so that we could now exercise it with angelic grace, amplifying the rest of those traits that give angels such a gratuitous place in our hearts? That is most assuredly a choice we can make now.

If we are ready to take responsibility for our own choices and hold them in the light of pure intention, we might carry the angelic frequency to a new and higher expression. In so doing, we will allow them to pass on to their own destiny as we free them from their human karma. The angels themselves seem willing to await our choice in the matter. They can stay and defend, protect and speak to us, or they can be freed to their own pressing evolutionary opportunities. If we are conscious enough to free them, the initiative for their release will certainly have to come from us as a gesture of our free will in its most enlightened application.

As our world goes through this extraordinary transition into a more enlightened era, it is difficult to perceive the importance of releasing the few good energies that preserve human hope. Yet it is crucial to recognize that we are a part of a larger whole, from which we can borrow and exchange in order to create new possibilities and potentials. Because we share genetic material with the angels, we can trust that we have those most magnificent attributes stored away inside us as well. We have projected all goodness onto angels and by comparison find ourselves to be their unworthy replicas. Only when we can view our world through the clear lens of spiritual awareness will we be able to find peace with all experience. We inherit from the angels the capacity for unconditional love, which they have learned through their own folly and experience. They could not hold the frequencies of light as they do if they were carrying Lucifer's karmic guilt by continuing to blame him. We bind them to it by praying for their protection (which they vowed to give us because of the Luciferian experience), rather than taking responsibility for ourselves. Instead, we could be reveling in the glory of communing with the angels on their octave. If we signal to them that we are ready to transmute the lower levels, they too are prepared to transcend to higher octaves.

Where would they go? I was given a breathtaking answer to this question in a session I did to clear the angels. It began with a quickening of the energy field within the uppermost astral strata of the celestial angelic kingdom:

"There is a strengthening of the Christed yellow-gold energy that prevails in the angelic realm, as if to prepare it for a transition. The celestial web of heaven's sky is opened and I look out to see the spinning of a spectacular galaxy. I find myself flowing through the opening into the energy field of light. It is the texture of satin and water, and I feel it caressing my very being. It is a completely new energy field into which the angels will ascend. We are translating from a carbon atom base to a silicon atom base. This spinning galaxy has a crystalline structure. The crystals are like powdery snowflakes, something with a million facets, as if blown by a fan. It is a different kind of light molecule."

My Higher Self says:

"As the sun is to the Earth in its golden light, this spiraling galaxic energy is to lightning, although there is no electrical charge.

"The powerful energy is spinning towards the astral strata of the angels, and it slaps into the upper strata like milk over the lip of glass and passes down through the Earth. It is an aspect of the photon belt that bombards our astral dimension, and after flowing through it, slides down into the third dimension. I realize that I have seen this alien light before in my most profound states of consciousness. The galaxic energy field is itself a spin point into another frequency, in which I take on a Light Body that is like an obelisk of very bright white light. It is like a warp field of light that is ironing space. It shifts the dimensions and opens the encapsulated spaces.

"As the galaxic energy penetrates the heavens, it encompasses the angels for their ascension. The beautiful translucent yellow-gold of the Christed light is freed by the increased vibrational velocity and it performs the transformation of the angelic DNA. It is a quality of joyousness that the Christed light gives to the angels that facilitates the transcendence. As this occurs there is a clearing of the angelic/ human karma. At first it appears like a vacuous amber, and as the interface between us dissolves, it becomes a powerful beam of Christed light. As if by the force of a laser, the form of "the smiting angel of God" explodes and an entire astral stratification from layers below dissolves, taking with it untold suffering and separation.

"The energy of infinite joy floods into my body and I feel the absolute link with the angelic frequencies. As a liquid pink pearl, they descend through the ninth and eighth chakras and spin the lotus of my crown chakra, spiraling through my eyes and all the way down as

a thin cocoon of light. Yes, we will always know where the angels are: in a spinning galaxy of crystal, which we will inherit one day, too!"

FREE THE ANGELS

The awareness of our need to free the angels came to me during one of my classes with the Nizhoni divinity students. We had been discussing karma from the holographic perspective of how cause and effect form a circle and reconnect to create a ripple of action and reaction that continues almost into infinity, merging the past and the future as like energies. Within the law of projection, we were viewing our separation from the Divine. We were working on the spiritual axiom that what is outside is always inside. In the same way that a negative characteristic of another person only bothers us if we are hiding or denying that same characteristic in ourselves, what we perceive as extraordinary and exquisite is also within us. Otherwise, we would have no way to perceive its existence. When we find those energies — both negative and positive — in ourselves, we become free of the karmic bondage from outside sources and both the outer world and the inner world are transformed.

I was using the case of the angels to make my point about how we are entrapping them because we cannot see that they are a part of us. I had pointed out that if we were brave enough to free them, in fact, we would become them. They would be very happy to help us accomplish this feat. The Earth and the sky would always have the angels. Their legacy would be strengthened and fixed to our genetic encoding to ensure that our new species will be one that carries the highest spiritual integrity. As I spoke, one of the students suddenly had the flash that we should make a sticker that said:

FREE THE ANGELS!

I have been speaking around the world about freeing the angels ever since. The results have been astounding. The realization that one can commune with the angels, not only receive messages or feelings, has had life altering effects on many people.

When queried about their purpose and their message, the angels have been very illuminating. I asked my students to converse with some of the angels and report back their conversations. Here are a few short excerpts I thought especially interesting:

"The angels came as a fast silver energy. They say that they are still here because they are so connected to the human heart. They open it up and are themselves nourished by it. My higher Self says that they open other spheres for us. We exchanged gifts to release them. They gave me apricot light which caused the sensation that my crown chakra was expanding. They asked me to give them a road. As they took it into them, they appeared to be standing in a very intense sky blue light."

(Exchange with four angels)

"We are messengers of love and we keep the gates open. ... We instill trust into the human heart, preparing mankind for the big leap."

(Gift exchange)

"The first angel gives me a pair of wings; the second gives me a bowl of translucent elixir for me to drink and purify myself; the third angel gives me a glowing sword to fight my demons, and the fourth gives me a seven-pointed crystal to hold the truth and the light on Earth.

"I give the first angel my eyes, to see and understand the world. The second one I give my arms and hands, so he can soothe the pain of the people. The third one I give my legs and feet, so he can withstand the power of ignorance through me, and to the fourth I surrender my ego, so he can use my humble instrument to do service in the world."

ARCHANGEL MICHAEL

(spreads his wings) *"I am here for the metamorphosis of the human race into the higher vibrations of light and divine love. … I am the messenger of the Light Body. I carry the energy of love and peace through which humans can recognize their true selves. I hold the sword of truth and the key of light."*

ARCHANGEL GABRIEL

"I am a gatekeeper attuned to the heart and to sound vibration. I am here to re-create the matrix of the heart chakra and to bring, teach, and uphold unconditional love. I facilitate joy, laughter, and play. I protect children in their awake and sleep states. I help them learn to read and write through the sound vibration."

With each communication, the students exchanged gifts with the angels to align their energies and move into the angelic frequency. I have spoken about this pattern in all of my books because it is so wonderful to actually feel the energies that are exchanged. The exchanges are always very personal in their symbology and form. Here is a lovely example:

(Gift exchange) *"I gave the angels a turquoise rain. It began to clear the pinky/white light that pervaded like a fog. Everything began to fold up, including pictures of Jesus, Mary, and others. It all disappeared, leaving a huge black hole that swallowed the universe story and our own creation story as well. Nothing. Silence. A black canvas. Then, like the eternal womb, it burst out with waters drenching me with new life. Excellent.*

"The angels gave me a gold disk, a watch without hands or face. They entered into my third eye. As they went in, for a flutter of a moment, I felt the featheriness of being an angel, the wings at the

shoulders, and the sensation of the feet. It awakened my angelic frequency. ... Then, a freshness and thankfulness. It is still with me."

One of my friends, a very powerful animal healer and artist who has always had angels around her, told me that freeing her angels has been one of the most terrifying and magical experiences of her life. She described how they have always surrounded her with their wonderful love and she wondered if she could live without their presence and love. She had always been a very psychic and sensitive child and they had helped her survive the suffering around her. She said that as I spoke about freeing the angels in one of my "knowings" classes, she felt the cold shivers all through her body and the hair standing up on the back of her neck that always occurs when something true and important happens. She went right home and into her garden filled with stars. Standing alone in the night, she asked her angels to come to her and tell her if they approved of this action. They expressed absolute ecstasy and bathed her in the most exquisite love, stroking and fanning her with their wings while she cried out her tears. She was encompassed in a soft pink glow and suddenly she felt the most amazing love pouring out of her in every direction. As she recounted her experience, I saw the golden edge of a halo around her head. Entranced by the softness of her eyes, I felt to be in the absolute and loving presence of a true angel.

The most powerful way to anchor the angelic frequency into the body is through the experience of it energetically. Though angelic lifetimes sometimes come up during normal Higher Self sessions, they more frequently appear when we are doing the Windows to the Sky and Soul Centering sessions. Just a glimpse into the higher astral regions of the celestial realms is enough to dissolve reams of self hatred, disdain, and judgment.

It is important to break the taboo against having direct contact with the Divine. Most religions have actively discouraged this as sacrilege or delusion since an appropriate intermediary has been designated as necessary. Either the religion has carefully selected those few who are "worthy" of the position, or a person must be trained for a long period of time to be ready for such a lofty task. The Nizhoni College of Divinity is focused on helping everyone anchor the Divine Source directly into their own body and consciousness. Since all of our genetic DNA holds the teachings of eons of religious endeavor, what is needed in today's world is the practice of living divinely. This need not be accomplished only through diligent discipline, but by rapturous, blissful infusion of spiritual awareness in every aspect of our lives.

When suddenly you discover that you are in an angelic body, having an angelic experience, it alters your vibration exponentially. Sometimes during a session, a person is reluctant or embarrassed to acknowledge themselves as such a magnificent being as an angel. When they finally experience the love and compassion they hold inherently from the angelic reality, they are quite overwhelmed. It is a frequency of our birthright that we have been missing out on for a long time.

Clearing karma with angels by awakening lifetime memories is an exquisite way to actually have a firsthand experience of the angelic frequency, so that it can be duplicated here in the third dimension. Here is a short experience of a writer who discovered herself in a simultaneous angelic episode:

I'm spinning and flying at the same time. Now I feel a gentle texture to the air, its a kind of sweetness. Someone is telling me, "Open your eyes, we are all here." I open my eyes and see a group of cherubs around me and one tall archangel a little distance off. They are playing lovely music on their harps and I, too, have a harp. They are laughing and saying, "Write something for us so we can spread your joy!"

Without a thought, I suddenly roll my hands in the air and wondrously, I have manifested an angel book. It is like reaching in and grabbing a pearl and bringing it out. It is a collection of human stories, humorous and profound. The story is told from the light of cosmic truth, illuminating the laws of karma. We hold what it will bring to the Soul and the moment of accomplishment; we applaud and cheer and play our harps.

The archangel begins to converse with me. It is such a familiar essence, almost as if it were my own. I venture the question, "Have I been you before?"

With a gentle smile he replied, "Yes." He wore the most gorgeous set of wings with an exquisite halo. He began to point out the different kinds of halos.

"When you are writing and manifesting the angel books, you have a dispersal of color flecks in your halo. You must use the opalescent white pearl halo, to give the highest gift."

We are conversing in a language of images. He shows me a long path with people expressing human emotion. The path continues on and we discuss what they can be shown at this time. I want to mix some star seeds in little reflecting ponds along the way. He says, "You can put some star essence into the mineral molecules."

The star seed, water, and light are mixed while I swirl the water to blend it so it can be put into human form.

"Will you help me?"

"Yes," he said, "but this will hurt a little bit and it must come through you."

I was trying to conceptualize any kind of pain that would be related to his energy, when the shock of a laser arrow with a sparkly tip suddenly penetrated down through the top of my head into the roof of my mouth to the base of my throat. Flashing sparks flew in every direction and my body began to disintegrate. As he slowly pulled the arrow out, it recomposed into a swirl of sparkles which then flowed out of the top. The angelic books poured in through the top, and I felt my body metamorphose into an angel of his stature.

"We will now open your angelic spin point into your human body so that you can experience that you are living in these two bodies simultaneously."

I felt a slight pressure just in front of the upper heart, under the throat. I became intensely aware of all the other angels gathering around. Laughingly, they nodded their approval.

"This is better for us all, you know. Want to try your wings?"

I can feel two huge wings wrapping around me and embracing my whole body.

"If you want to jump off, they will open. Try it!"

I do and, instantly, I am flying towards the sun. There is a smiling golden light moving through me, and I know I can bring this into my task of manifestation on Earth.

Now is the time for us all to awaken the angelic frequency. The window of evolution is coming into view, and we may claim the next rung of the ladder that is such a catapultic leap up for us that we will experience an entirely new reality.

Many of our children and children's children will come into embodiment through the angelic spin points. They will be angels from the beginning. Their wings might not be external, functional, or symbolic appendages, but they will be the wings of consciousness. They will take flight into a millennium of enlightened and free beings. We will have done our part by anchoring in the angelic frequencies through our intense spiritual awakening.

The angels are inviting us to enter their domain; they are not asking us to bring them physically into ours, except through our own bodies. We must attain "heaven on Earth" by raising our vibration to open the veil between our simultaneous dimensions. The angels are preparing us to look upward, not to project onto them but to be inspired to reach for all that they represent within ourselves. What do you project onto them? Is it purity, unwavering faith, absolute love? Somewhere within you, you hold the seeds of such possibilities. If you find them within yourself, you will free the angels.

Ask your body where you hold those qualities. Imagine that you are opening the capsule that contains them and allowing them to flood through you, imprinting the energy in each of your cells.

If you begin to meditate on the angelic frequency, you will be able to recognize it everywhere around you. Go to any crowded place and look for an angel. You will find one, visible or invisible, peeking out from quiet eyes in smiling faces. As you engage with strangers and friends, treat them as if they truly are angels and you are having a divine moment with them ... and they will be!

The human emotional body never lets go of anyone unless it feels there is someone else to take the other's place. In this case, it is not a "someone" but a frequency: an all-encompassing and loving frequency that creates a new kind of space in which we absolutely know that we are not alone any longer.

When you are ready to free the angels, it will be most helpful to exchange gifts so that you experience the energy inside you. Simply ask the angels to take form. It may be one particular race of angels that comes forth or it might be an individual, such as a Guardian angel, or a group. Ask them to give you a gift so that you can carry their frequency. It may be a symbol, an object, or a color.

When you perceive it, take it into your body and focus carefully on recording how it comes in and that it is carried into all of your cells. This will activate the angelic resonance within your DNA structure.

In this way, we create heaven on Earth by living both at once and joining their unique qualities. We are capable of finding focus in more than one dimension simultaneously, and yet being fully present synergistically in both. As we discover the spin points that converge these energies, we will find that the human experiment is one worthy of our choice.

THE PRACTICAL HALO

I lay there beneath my star ceiling, watching the Milky Way stretch itself out like a cosmic highway. I was reviewing the sessions I had listened to this evening in the Soul Centering workshop. Why, I wondered, are we so afraid of trying out our wings and living the strength and beauty that is ours? I smiled to myself as I thought about the exquisite angelic experience one person had described in a simultaneous lifetime. Did she understand what it meant to have these energies moving through her Earth body? If she let that angel be visible, her whole life would change.

It is so hard to hold those lofty thoughts. We have such good intentions, but they yield almost without a struggle to the more common doubts and judgments. How could we hold our goodness just a little longer?

I thought about how I prepare for my "Knowings" class on Tuesday nights. As I meditate, I say a little prayer or mantra: "Let me be the instrument." I feel the energy of my Higher Self encompass me and I know my auric field becomes much larger and more beautiful. I am especially aware of its radiance above my head. It is as if I were creating a halo to remind others of who we truly are.

Often, people will say, "I've always wanted to see auric fields and tonight, for the first time, I saw yours. It's like a big beautiful halo."

As I watched the stars, I thought of how the radiance of the celestial bodies is very like a halo. If we focused on creating the phenomenon of a halo, our vibration and even our consciousness would be elevated to those same octaves. The wonderful resonance of my Higher Self interrupted my contemplation with three words: **"The Practical Halo."**

"That's it!" I gasped.

I had never considered the possibility that we could manifest halos through our intention, in the same way that I work on my entire energy field when I am going to speak. The halo is an energetic phenomena. It could be consciously activated, just like quickening the auric field. With great joy, I envisioned a room full of people wearing halos. Initially, it would be a bit of "The Emperor's New Clothes," in that not everyone could see the halos, but seeing them might be even easier than perceiving the auric field, because they are so concentrated. Everyone would feel the haloic presence in and around them, but the most difficult part would be to convince ourselves that we are capable and deserving of the halo.

Halos have come to represent divine perfection in the sense of a permanent state of being. Therefore, we humans have always felt it to be out of our reach, since our sacred moments seem very fleeting. It has been deeply imbedded into our genetic material that we are not a direct part of the Divine, that we are separate and have no right to claim a part of it. We have been taught that only certain chosen people can manifest miracles and wear halos.

All those who have performed miracles have been called saints and wore the wings of angels, or are called impostors or aliens. A miracle is something we cannot comprehend. It is beyond our technology and our sphere of consciousness, but it is not beyond the knowing of our Higher Self. Everyone on this planet has accessed these frequencies in at least one incarnation, as well as through the experiences of Soul friends. We have been asked to be the miracle makers and we can't remember that we know how, or that we have divine permission to do it. It is not surprising that we do not feel capable of performing miracles when we have lost the capacity or, perhaps, the desire to see the good in each other.

Many people might feel that a halo would be a terrible burden because you would have to continually defend yourself against making mistakes. The inner dialogue concerning worthiness would be too stultifying in terms of proof of holiness, or being able to give up the world. The halo does not keep you from being in the world. In fact, it will create a new world to live in. It simply eclipses your separation from your true self, so that the lightness is able to move in and through you, if only in spurts. Everyone is capable of this and touches it at some moment of their lives.

Even the saints do not manifest the halo constantly, because of the fluctuations in their own emotions. Their divine acts come, not because they never feel doubt or anger, but because of their spiritual strength and courage to pass up through these energies into higher octaves.

We must discover that we, too, have that kind of strength. My Higher Self said, "You need something physical for the consciousness to grasp. The halo is an energetic, electromagnetic, and biochemical phenomenon that can help you to hold your consciousness, your hopes and dreams, onto a high enough level that you can make the catapultic leap from where you are now, with your separation and your struggles, to who you were born to be: Beings of Light."

With this comment, my Higher Self began one of its beautiful teachings about the art of the halo. An array of beings flowed through my visual field, wearing their halos. Some identified themselves as saints and martyrs, angels, and even Light Beings from other dimensions. I was shown several different kinds of halos such as the golden halo, and the large, more diffused white halo.

I was told that the halo is a window to other dimensions. When our energies are strong enough to call down the currents, they interface with our own light pulses to create the halo. The cosmic laws of energy carried by those currents allow a natural effect which we call miracles.

Let me share this brief excerpt from a session of a person doing the Windows to the Sky series at The Light Institute:

"I am in a meeting of Elders. We are discussing the preparation of the boy for his travels to the Far East, where we will send him to finish his initiations with the Masters of Light.

"We are a group of seven. Each has passed the initiation of the first light chakra above the physical, which bestows the Golden Halo on the physical body. I begin, 'The little miracles, he has performed since a small child.'"

"True. But he still treats them like childish play."

"Exactly. Yesterday, I saw him restore a bird to life and when I queried him about the rules for such an act, he only smiled at me and said, 'God said so!'"

"How can we instill discipline in someone whose haloic light is stronger than any of ours?"

"Yes. We're supposed to anchor in the golden frequencies so that he will use the human form, and there he is jumping ahead into the white."

"I say we should keep him working physically so that he knows the meaning of sweat on his body."

"He's too young for carnal sweat. Besides, the way he loves wood, he might start making life forms out of it!"

"I'm more concerned about that halo. We can't let him go wandering about. People will start gathering around him before we can finish our task."

"Don't worry, there is so much density out there. No one will even see it."

"People will feel it. They need miracles and they will know that he can do them."

"Yes. If we overplay this physical thing, he may start sharing the teachings so that everyone can transcend their body."

"They'll never understand that law."

"But it would be like him to try to show it to them. That would be a disaster. They would surely kill him for it!"

The lifetime went on in breathtaking revelation. Descriptions of haloic practices were brought forth, and activated in the present body. We sparked the DNA matrix to further awaken the energy of the halo so that all humans might also begin to feel its presence in their genetic encoding. I cannot help but wonder what is happening to this person now — perhaps miracles!

If we could begin to practice the energy levels necessary to construct our halos, they would serve as an anchor of the light into the human body. This could be a very practical response to the difficulties we are having today on Planet Earth. A body that holds a halo must have a frequency that includes conscious illumination, peace, and bliss. Imagine the quality of our communications, if they occurred while we were accessing these haloic channels!

Even if we can only hold the halo energy for a short moment, we will be teaching our body to recognize different frequencies that will help it to return to them, ever more easily. The physical body is the bridge, the gateway, to our other bodies and their energies. Through the activation of the master glands, we can begin to create the biochemical and electromagnetic forces needed for the halo.

The pituitary, hypothalamus, and pineal glands all hold essence material that provides the link into the Light Body. The pineal gland is the lens and the threshold for light frequencies into the body. If the halo is to be functioning, there must be some opening of the third eye, stimulated by the retinic cells of the pineal gland. It is most important to work with the triad of master glands so that they can function on both physiological and Light Body levels. In my book and video, *The Ageless Body,* I demonstrate how to activate their sacred nectar by breathing color into them.

The haloic energy is to the astral body as the astral body is to the physical body. When we wear halos, it causes our frequencies to shift upward. A halo is the energy field of the Light Body, just as the aura is the energy field of the physical body. This means that the light frequencies of the halo are faster than those of the astral, in the same way that the astral body is lighter than the physical body. Even though the saints may dwell in the angelic kingdom at the highest level of the astral dimension, the frequencies of light that produce the halo come from even higher universal levels. What we think of as heaven is in the astral. There are worlds beyond our scope of imagining.

It might be easier to perceive the different energies in a vertical format. Imagine the crown chakra as the culmination of all the chakric energies of the body. In India, it is seen as the thousand-petaled lotus. It is like a fountain that releases the energy from the top of the head. Cascading down around the body, it is swept up again through the feet, completing one full cycle of energy. When we include the energy centers of our subtle bodies, such as the astral and Light bodies, we see that our holographic human design has coalescing points of reference above the body that are intrinsic to its whole. We not only have the seven major chakras of the body, but we have an eighth and ninth chakra that correspond to our spiritual blueprint. The eighth and ninth chakras extend the height of our energy field, while channeling the energies in toward us. They are gathering the higher astral and cosmic energies that expand our conscious realities, and synergistically anchoring them into us.

Perhaps, if we can experience these energies in our bodies, we will finally understand how magnificent it is to fabricate a vehicle of light, with which to express the Soul. The light energies manifest themselves through the brilliance of the halo and they are locked into the encoding of our DNA. Even if the halo has not been activated until this moment, its potential is always there waiting for us to reach it. There are special spin points that act like spinning vortices, gathering them in so that they are accessible to our bodies. All of this happens through the power of these chakras above the head, which are a part of the subtle strands of human source and destiny.

You can discover for yourself the spin points to your haloic energy. In a meditative state, breathe deeply into your body and ask it to show you where you are carrying the spin point that links you to your halo. You may sense a great expansion of light in the area of the spin point. Release your consciousness into the energy and allow yourself to be completely absorbed. This helps you to become accustomed to the higher frequencies so that you are comfortable passing in and out of the vortices.

Connecting with the haloic energy is not the same as going out of body through your astral body into the astral dimension, while leaving your physical body lying there. When you connect with the haloic energy, you are lifting up the vibration of the physical body so that it is transcends into higher light frequencies. There is not the vague sense of having dreamed it, but rather it is a very vibrant state of clarity. This may be why it is so difficult to hold the energy for any length of time. We must train our cells to maintain their integrity in such frequencies. Fortunately, each time you experience it, cellular memory (from this and other bodies) will help to anchor it in as a holographic reference, even for a flicker of a moment.

We have always looked upward to that which is above us. In our paintings and sculptures, we depict inspired beings reaching into the heavens to connect with and receive something that lifts them from a lonely existence. Since we have an innate sense that the Divine enters and exits out of the top of the head, we have created the gamut of simple to extraordinary headpieces to represent those energies; the visible symbols remind us of our spiritual realities.

In almost all societies, those of special status wear a hat or some sacred article on their heads to symbolize the authority and power of higher energies. The hat or article signifies the ability of the person wearing it to make contact with something only the wearer of that hat can do. Consider the many religious hats that convey those higher connections: there are the hats of the Pope, the bishops, the cardinals; there are the ceremonial pieces such as the Buddhist's Black Hat ceremony; the feathered headdresses of chiefs and shamans; the turbans of the Sikhs, headwraps of the Muslims, Arabians and Turks, skullcaps of the Jews, the hats of the Hassidics, and on into almost every group on the planet.

The power of the pharaohs and kings were depicted by their headpieces. The pointed hat of the magician, and even the hats worn by university professors and graduating students to convey a certain mastery of knowledge — all express the relationship of the head with other realms. The hats worn by judges, policemen, warriors, and even brides signal to the onlookers that these are special people. Different groups have shaved their heads, tattooed them, covered their heads, or even worn their hair on top of the head to create a look communicating that the head represents their special status and must be protected. The Egyptians, Tibetans, Incas, Mayans, and Aztecs all altered the shape of the head or performed specific operations to create a visual sense of heightened consciousness.

As we open our awareness to the higher chakras, we will access the very energies these groups have been seeking to express symbolically through the body. What could be more practical than an energetic halo that is part of ourselves and yet part of the whole universe? Our halo is available to us in any place and at any time. The Windows to the Sky are opening now, and we must look up and out through them until we find exactly that of the Divine which pertains to us, and anchor it into our human experience.

WINDOWS TO THE SKY

The re-discovery of the Windows to the Sky was like a coming home for me. All my life I had kissed Death and run away; six times I crossed over and back from someplace I remembered only in my submerged feelings. It was like counting coup, Indian style. Touching the Enemy is much more illuminating than killing him. So I played at the edge of the veil, glimpsing the sparks of something that was reflected in my eyes. Oh yes, I had been there ... many times.

The Windows flooded into view through a five thousand-year-old memory. They were used then, to facilitate the priests and elite on secret journeys into the cosmos for the expansion of their consciousness, and to "anchor the Sky" back into their Earth bodies. Through my knowledge of energy pathways, I had been their instrument. At first, as the memories resurfaced, all I could hold of the Windows were the sensations of moving in and out of dimensions and worlds seemingly unattached to ours, at unthinkable velocity.

In those nebulous times, only a few were prepared to venture into the unmanifest. Now there are many, and the urgency is pressing in on us like a birthing of ourselves and our planet. We are in the final stage of transition, before the last few pushes bring forth a fantastic leap into a more enlightened world. If we open the Windows to the Sky, the peace and clarity of other dimensions will enter into ours.

At The Light Institute, we lead people into other-dimensional experiences through a process we call "Soul Centering." Soul Centering is an expansive venturing into the realms of other dimensions, guided by the Higher Self. The energies are anchored back into the body so that the illumination we experience can be utilized in our present reality. Soul Centering lifts the emotional body up into the higher realms of expression, allowing us to remember the exquisite feelings of oneness that emanate from the Soul.

We must integrate all that we know and dream about our purpose in the cosmos. We cannot limit ourselves to the third dimension and hope to play our part in the evolutionary scheme. That which was once considered impractical fantasy must now be put to the test as we practice our true capacities. We must reach into the invisible worlds to pass this initiation of illumination, and we must do it now!

I began opening the Windows to the Sky in the same way I had 5,000 years ago: through the focus of golden acupuncture needles, placed in the esoteric points. They form very specific geometric patterns in a circuitry of currents. I never fully accepted the necessity to prick the point in order to activate it. This creates the illusion that the acupuncturist is causing the effect, when, in fact, the person is using the stimulus as a catalyst to energies already present within. I soon stopped using the needles altogether, in favor of the person stimulating the points with light. This way, they can trust that they are actually doing it themselves.

Opening the Windows now, in contrast to thousands of years ago, has shown me that the separation between mind and body is infinitely greater today than it was then. I realized that we could not simply translate these polluted bodies into the light frequencies, because they have been so abandoned. Their owners have lost their capacity to commune with them and have strayed into their minds for company. We will have to re-ignite the fires of the body and awaken the cellular memory if we are to gain access to the kind of expansion necessary for this higher work.

Today, there is a dangerous trend of escaping the body through drugs, which creates a profound emotional separation, not only from our own bodies, but from true relationship with others who share our world. With alarming casualness, people around the planet are turning to drugs to pull away the veil, exposing other realities that seem more lucid than the foggy monotony of real life. Too many people have seen into the "Beyond" to deny its existence, but this passivity of viewing creates an external source of awareness. Though they may catch a glimpse of heaven or hell, the price is long term damage to their auric field and genetic material. The wobble of spectator reality ripples out through the subtle bodies and immobilizes the spirit. We need to have these experiences, but we need to participate in them through our own creativity and will.

There is a way to design a holographic progression of spiritual illumination without excessive wobble. The Windows to the Sky sessions at The Light Institute help the person charge their body with the cosmic currents, that in turn guide its consciousness back out into octaves and dimensions which are otherwise too different for the body to perceive. Because the energy circuits become fused, the person going through the experience can hold the energies and feel what it is to be Light, without losing contact with this world.

My Higher Self showed me how to align the consciousness of the *kundalini* and *shakti* life force energies to the upper chakras. In this way, the subtle body currents can be anchored into the physical so as to bring integration, rather than separation, to the person. By entering into the kundalini nadi, we can clear karmic interference with the upward flow of the kundalini, returning it to its home in the upper chakras.

After we work with the kundalini, we move into the octaves of the eighth and ninth chakras, which are the golden and silver-white chakras, respectively. These are connecting worlds of such light and intensity, it may be hard to imagine that they can be integrated into ours. They are the realms of synergistic realities, frequencies of light beyond our spectrum and encounters with other beings who have learned the cosmic laws of energy and therefore wield a technology that could be of great value to us.

When you read the vignettes of experiences in these upper octaves, you may wonder how a person could use them in our reality, since they are often so removed from form and structure. It is the **energy** that is of such transformative value to us. When a person has been able of their own volition to attain these frequencies, they become larger than life and so their very presence is uplifting to others.

THE EIGHTH CHAKRA

Golden Chakra

The eighth chakra is called the golden chakra because it is spun on the golden threads of the matrix of matter. Gold is the color of form and manifestation. It creates structure and holds the intersecting links of the cosmic web. The gold frequencies lift us up into higher realms that support our true humanity. The Christed energy, with its exquisite yellow-gold light, encompasses the golden chakra. Its radiance is not the aura of the human body per se. It is a radiance of the higher astral and celestial fields.

The golden chakra begins one or two feet above the head. It is the first leap off the physical body. After the ray energy of the crown chakra, there is a seemingly empty space for those few feet and then the golden chakra can be located as a strong energy vortex at about arm's length above the head. It is incredible to contemplate that something which does not touch our physical body could be a part of us, and yet it is. It is connected to our spiritual DNA which intertwines our physical DNA. When we raise our vibration, the golden chakra is activated and begins to spin. As it does, it becomes a channel that coalesces higher energies into its center. It is attracted to our field and when it reaches the spraying arch of the crown chakra, it bends around it to create the golden halo.

There are many ways to help yourself prepare for the golden halo. It is important to desire and intend its presence in your life because once you experience it, there will be many changes that occur as a result of its profound effect on you. Calling down the golden halo can be done in meditation and prayer, once you can quicken your frequencies to reach up to it. You must call its energy from the most lighted part of yourself, but don't feel that you have to be a saint to attempt it. Now is the perfect moment, not some nebulous future when you think you will be perfect.

What you eat does make a difference. You are inviting pure light to surround and enter you and it is good to give your cells a diet of living foods, rich in chlorophyll, so that they do not respond to increased light by detoxing. I feel that everyone on the planet should be eating some form of blue-green algae because it was the first organism to translate sunlight into life. It is one of the most ancient and successful planetary life forms that began before the ozone layers protected us from radiation. As the radiation levels are now rapidly increasing, we need to use blue-green algae as a buffer until our own bodies can adjust.

Let me show you how to focus your energies to create the necessary frequency for a halo. There are several things to do first that will get the fields moving:

The quickest shift in your energy will come from spinning. Try to spin for as long as you can. Whether it is only a few times around or many, it will free both your mind and your body from the kind of holding on that keeps you from higher perception. Sit down and close your eyes.

Breath is the next step to quicken your energy. The *pranayama* fire breath is an excellent technique for synchronizing the master gland triad. It is done by "snorting" strongly out through the nose on exhalation. Begin slowly and increase to rapid successions (like the sound of a train going faster and faster) for a few breaths and then slowing down to a stop. Take a deep breath and squeeze up your pubicoxegeous muscle (around the anus) as you exhale your breath. This will send the energy up into the third eye, in the center of your forehead.

At the back of the nose is a membrane covering the hole into the brain and directly behind it is the pituitary gland. The fire breath will vibrate the membrane and stimulate the master glands. You may feel a bit light-headed after this exercise, or you may feel an ache in the middle of your forehead, over the third eye. All of this is perfectly normal. Now you are ready to begin the special breathing that brings you into contact with the golden chakra.

Switch your attention to the top of your head and breathe deeply in and out several times. You may have a sensation of fizzing or buzzing around your crown chakra; this is good.

Use your breath like a laser. Breathe in through your third eye and breathe out through your crown chakra, lasering your energy upward until you sense a connection with the golden chakra. Remember that it is about the length of your arm above your head. Do not breathe for a moment while you are sensing this golden center; then breathe in through the golden chakra, down and out your third eye.

Do this a series of times while you are imagining yourself encompassed in the golden light. Soon you will feel a kind of full-ness around your head, especially over the top and on the sides. This is the haloic frequency coming into your energy field. Prac-tice this again and again until you can create the sensation easily with your breath and your conscious intention. Do the exercise when you are going out, so that you have the sensation of literally wearing your halo. Just imagining carrying a halo is a giant step for anyone. If you even pretend you have a halo, the rest of your auric field will align to that octave and you will begin to experience a new sense of harmony and joy.

One of my advanced Divinity students was working on this and told a funny story about it later in class. After feeling a strong sensation of the golden halo around her, she went downtown to practice carrying it as she walked along. She said that she was very surprised to discover that not only did no one appear to notice it, but she felt totally invisible. People seemed to look right through her without seeing her at all. As she walked through the park, a drunk suddenly came towards her and holding his hands up at the sides of his head like a halo, he laughingly said, "You're shining! Just keep shining!"

I, too, have noticed that children and sensitive people are the ones who turn around to look again at my head. Sometimes I see their halo and a look of recognition passes between us. It is not something between a child and an adult, or between strangers; it is the knowing embrace of two Souls!

There are angels on Earth who are conscious of their purpose and destiny, and there are those who carry the angelic DNA who have not yet discovered themselves. Here is an excerpt of one woman's revelation as a result of connection to her golden chakra:

"*I perceive the golden chakra like a fountain. It feels as if it were flowing down into and through me. As it comes into me, it washes away a lot of old karma and I feel a tremendous sense of lightness.*

"*The golden light moves into my throat, through to the back and spreads out at the bottom and top of my spine. ... It's coming out the top of my head like an umbrella with bundles of fibers, each of which has a bulbous star at its tip. The umbrella is coming from the golden chakra and is connected to the angels. Their halos are like golden filigree, with blue and white light radiating through.*

"As I gaze at them, a deep recognition starts to stir in me. We are old friends. I feel their love for me and I realize that we are working together. As they smile at me, I have the revelation that I am one of them. ... I am an angel having a human experience!

"It's as if I have taken a small part of me, like the tip of my little finger, and placed it into a human incarnation. The purpose of this is to give a gift to the evolution of the humans. We're all (the angels and I) doing this together. It requires rapt attention, yet only from the one small part of my being. The rest is focused here with the angels. I have a tremendous amount of courage to do this.

"I am getting a message. It says the light is inside me. It is fluid. There's no external source. I'm perpetual. I have a wonderful feeling of timeless, ageless, inevitable wholeness."

Here is another person's experience of the golden chakric energy:

"I am sitting under an olive tree playing the flute. The music moving through me is the frequency of the golden chakra, and it comes into my body and out of my mouth. It radiates all around me. The DNA holds the energy and causes an expansion of my field. It feels so warm and there is a sense of unlimited abundance, riches of golden light. The golden light needs a reflection to embrace its truth; otherwise, it just permeates and goes through without any visibility. Together with my flute, I become its reflection, and I extend up like an antenna that reaches into the higher octaves and calls forth the golden energy.

"The antenna is like a crown, open at the top, but floating above my head. There is a hole at the bottom that is variable and as big as the diameter of the body. On the top of the crown is a funnel, comparatively shallow, and it is antenna and funnel at the same time. The antenna is collecting the golden light and then it funnels it into the body like a waterfall.

"There is no tiredness and the resources are unlimited and abundant. ... Only through the antenna does it become manifest. In the moment that the antenna is active, it receives abundant and unlimited light energy and at that point, others can see it, too.

"It is contagious. In contact with humans, they feel immediately well and their chakras are simultaneously activated. If there is someone who sucks energy like a vampire, they are flooded with the light and so gifted that they cannot suck anymore. The golden light dissolves all the negative vibrations immediately and painlessly and that is why it is so connecting.

"The DNA reacts as if it were singing in harmony with the flute. This is the energy of ecstatic joy. It changes everything into gold. Every cell is exploding with life force energy. There is no need for will, purpose, direction, beginning, or ending. The light encompasses everything. There is only surrender. There is no question anymore because the answer is born of the question. No fear, just pure life.

"I feel other cosmic energies coming in now through the antenna. I see them as silver and red. They bring connections with other dimensions and realities.

"My Inner Child is laughing and it feels like a festival. He is telling me that my whole life is going to change. He whispers to me that the wisdom of the golden chakra is to accept and love everything that is happening."

All of these experiences into higher realms have been met with great depth of feeling. There are no words that could adequately convey the meaning they have for those who have been touched by them. Imagine a face of enraptured bliss, a voice softened by the expanse of the universe, a mind stilled by the infinite sea of oneness.

Without drugs, in full consciousness — by sound, with pulse, in light, and by visions strange and wondrous, they have found a place of resonance inside an inner universe and outside the confines of this dimension. Gently, quietly, they have changed.

What do they bring back for us? It is nothing we can hold in our hand. We must reach into the space of their ecstatic hearts and touch a point of essence. They have seen beyond, gone beyond a place that we both share, into worlds of their own. Because they have done this, we can do it too. We are free to find a point of source, to travel through the spheres and anchor those unfathomable energies directly into our bodies, our blood crystals, our DNA.

THE NINTH CHAKRA

Silver/White Chakra

To enter the funnel of the ninth chakra is to leave the scope of manifest matter and ascend into the swirling cosmic ethers. The laws of energy may allow for appearing form, which behaves within its purpose and again dissolves.

The silver-white chakra is the cloak of the Light Body. Its aura is one of white radiance, that sizzles around its nebulous form like an amorphous cocoon.

"Are you there?" I whispered.

"Yes. My silver-white chakra is like a silver liquid light, sparked with fire.

"I see egg shapes of luminescent light. I sense there are beings inside them. I stick my hand into them. They are filled with life.

"My cells are listening, communicating with that energy. They are so enthralled that all my cells are chattering at once.

"I am seeing hundreds of these beings hovering over a planet. It's in our solar system. It has a dust-like surface and within it are ice-cube structures with gas bubbles in them.

"I am again within the silver-white chakra, which has become a clear liquid. I am standing on its wetness.

"There is now a different kind of light. It is radioactive. It moves in square spirals, like those the Mayans drew.

"I see a face with a brown spot on the left cheek. It is a message about radiation in the body.

"I'm shown the vibration of the silver-white chakra. When it enters the face, the particles become like the fuzz in the universe.

"Though the body dissolves, experiences stay within the molecules. They look like a million pricks of light. They hold the experiences, which are then spread out through the matrix and are picked up by bodies coming through.

"I am bringing my body into the silver-white chakra. I feel a magnetic pulse in my hands and a different energy in my forehead and top of the head. ... I feel the molecules of my body shifting. It is a cold, rather metallic energy coming over my body. It is good. I am adjusting to the DNA of the silver-white energy. The Window to the Sky points are like large rainbow size arcs, not colored, but light. Like a hose spraying up in an arc, the droplets move into several simultaneous dimensions at once. They are the spin points and I, too, can move into those dimensions, if I choose.

"The fuzzy white pulsing light comes into my eyes and I open them as wide as possible so they can fit the flat cellular bubbles, like fast spinning wheels coming into my head. I am looking at the mechanism of the universe. Those are the same bubbles that showed me the secrets of life in one of my death experiences. My third eye area is chilled and I feel the tension above my head as the ninth chakra spins me out into space. ...

"My Higher Self gives me a tool to help me use the silver-white frequency. It looks like a horizon. It appears as a forest fire of brilliant white curly tongues of fire. It connects from the lotus of the crown chakra to the ninth chakra. It causes the silver-white energy to bend down around me. It pours down through my whole body, creating a misty space inside. Brilliant, brilliant white light.

"Suddenly, I am experiencing a reference point to the blue of the Shivic, Krishna energy. I feel as if my whole body is turning that same blue. I see the golden arc around the Krishna figure. It slips into me like a pure liquid, through the meditation point.

"I am receiving supernovas, swirling gases. They spread out and form invisible cities of liquid glass. They flow around the planet becoming moving colonies of a gel-like substance that protect Earth. My body has spread out too, like the horizon. I see the fringes of the flames, very white now. I am holding the fringes of the silver-white chakra around me like a giant sail. I feel a pulse like radiation. I am within a cloak of radiance!"

It was an exquisite moment as I watched her make contact with her silver-white chakra.

"What does it feel like?" I asked.

"God," she whispered.

The room was filled with the gentlest white light, pulsing softly in a way that found me holding my breath so as not to disturb its presence.

"What's happening now?" I asked gently.

"I am being infused with light. ... I hear sounds. Not celestial or Earth sounds. It's the hum of the universe!"

"What are you feeling?"

"I'm feeling the hum inside me. ...Wait! ... I am the hum!"

Silence... Space...

"What are you experiencing now?

"Velocity. So fast that it is standing still at the same time. Silver white light. I am being spun through it. I am being taken to the seam between the universes. It's a curving gesture, an arch without time.

"A sense of texture. ... They enfold one to the other.

"I can't step across, I am guided through. It's a nuance of a hand, yet there are no bodies. Its directional towards me because I am occupying space.

"It is my consciousness that has a point of reference ... No size or circumference, but a center. It is the center of my Soul!"

FLUIDITY

The infinite Soul sits within the center of consciousness. If you can feel its breath upon you, you will know intrinsically the purpose of your life. Consciousness is absolute fluidity. It is attached nowhere, yet it is your Source and you command it. You can ride the currents of the universe through your consciousness and touch all possibility. By reaching up into the centers of illumination, you can recognize your true self through all its bodies. Your presence there is a gift of guidance for Soul friends everywhere.

Let me inspire you to open the windows of consciousness onto a new world of liquid light, where truth and peace flow in and out of the heart of humans, over the river of life, on the rapids of absolute joy!

All that ripples in the etheric flows into us, and all that happens to us flows back into the liquid cosmic sea. We are not spectators in a game of winners and losers; we are the players and adventurers in the evolutionary universe. We are ourselves the flow.

Our sky is a magnificent part of our essence. As well as being the skin that encompasses our Earth and that breathes out into our solar neighborhood, it is the medium of our destiny. If we shift up our consciousness, we will realize that we are half the sky. It is not above us. It is *in* us. We are space and light and air. We are the hum of the atom, the carbon of Earth, the face of the Divine.

★ ★ ★ ★ ★ ★ *We are Soul Bodies.* ★ ★ ★ ★ ★ ★

CHRIS GRISCOM

Chris Griscom is a visionary and a spiritual teacher of global stature. Her great love for the Earth and all its peoples has prompted her to travel throughout the world, reminding us all of the sacredness of life. Her teachings and exercises in consciousness have been encapsulated in ten books, translated into ten languages, and read by millions across the globe. As the founder of The Light Institute of Galisteo and The Nizhoni School for Global Consciousness, Chris has guided people of all ages towards developing a relationship with their Higher Selves and inspired them to seek the meaning of life and to share their gifts with the world.

THE LIGHT INSTITUTE OF GALISTEO

Seekers around the world are attracted to the profound healing offered at The Light Institute of Galisteo. The Light Institute process centers on clearing the Emotional Body, the part of us which holds feelings and experiences from our childhood and our many incarnations. In a sacred and peaceful environment, clients are guided through a wonderful journey, which introduces them to their Inner Child, their Higher Self, and their own brilliance. Each session is specifically tailored for the highest growth for the participant. The Light Institute facilitators come from around the globe. After extensive inner work and training with Chris, the Light Institute facilitators guide participants through sessions with themes such as "Clearing the Parents," "Sexuality," and "Sense of Success." These are just some of the many themes explored at The Light Institute, in both an individual and group intensive format.

THE NIZHONI SCHOOL
FOR
GLOBAL CONSCIOUSNESS

"Nizhoni" is a Navajo word which means "The Beauty Way," a way in which everything is in balance in the hologram of life. The Nizhoni School of Global Consciousness offers a new form of education which allows people of all ages, from around the world, to discover their inner wisdom and to bring it forth to heal, teach, and lead. Founded in 1989 by Chris Griscom, Nizhoni is a holographic approach to education which helps us to find our place in the world and to see the interconnectedness of all experience and knowing. Nizhonis of all ages learn about their physical and subtle bodies, as well as the laws of energy the govern the manifest and unmanifest worlds.

Nizhoni students are taught to commune with their divine Higher Self so that they learn to trust their own inner voice. Freedom, clarity, and compassionate loving are the result. This "Soul-centered" education embraces the essential core of our humanness and teaches us how to access our highest potential and life purpose.

Nizhoni includes an international boarding and day school for primary grade and higher education students. It exemplifies conscious living, which provides a practical arena for the brilliance and extraordinary creativity that are unleashed by the Higher Self. The Emotional Body is uplifted to add ecstasy and joy to the experience of embodiment, in concert with the Soul. Nizhoni truly is "The Beauty Way"!

For more information about THE LIGHT INSTITUTE ("Inner Child," "Higher Self," and past life sessions; cranial sessions; workshops and programs; books and tapes), write, call, or fax:

The Light Institute
HC 75, Box 50
Galisteo, NM 87540 USA
Telephone (505) 466-1975
Fax (505) 466-7217

For more information about THE NIZHONI SCHOOL FOR GLOBAL CONSCIOUSNESS (two- or four-year "College of Divinity" program; one-year program, "The Nizhoni Experience"; Middle School; short programs for adults; summer camps for children, students, and adults), write, call, or fax:

The Nizhoni School for Global Consciousness
HC 75, Box 72
Galisteo, NM 87540 USA
Telephone (505) 466-4336
Fax (505) 466-7217

E-mail: nizhoni@nets.com

We are also on the Internet: http://www.nets.com/nizhoni

BOOKS AND TAPES
BY
CHRIS GRISCOM

═══ *Books* ═══

The Ageless Body revolutionizes the traditional concept of body time that determines how we grow old and die. No matter what age you are, you can help your body to become "ageless," enabling you to live with purpose and mastery. $15

Ecstasy Is New Frequency opens a pathway to our Higher Self and takes us through a quickened healing of the Emotional Body, to make way for the Soul. Ecstasy is living with the Soul in the body. $10

Healing of Emotion: Awakening the Fearless Self provides breathing techniques, visualizations with color, and consciousness-expanding exercises that allow us to truly awaken the fearless self. $10

Ocean Born: Birth as Initiation is an intimate and touching photographic account of the birth of Chris' sixth child in the ocean waters of the Bahamas (hard cover). $25

Quickenings: Meditations for the Millenium "... merging our consciousness in meditation ... amplifies its effect so that it echoes out ... to bring in a New World in which we can live and be at peace." $4

Nizhoni: The Higher Self in Education examines how "through the grace of the Higher Self, children can be taught 'knowing' from within the self and apply that knowing from a place of joy and enlightenment. This should be the goal of education." $10

Time Is an Illusion describes Chris' spiritual journey and the foundation of the Light Institute philosophy. Chris teaches readers how to begin a life-changing dialogue with the Higher Self. $10

 Video Tapes

The Ageless Body This video offers you a one-on-one experience with Chris Griscom, as you are guided to truly commune with your body. Come to know the secret functions of the endocrine system, and learn the gentle and effective Tibetan and Taoist exercises that will inspire a whole new physical consciousness within you. $30 (PAL $40)

Death and Samadhi Filmed in 1983, Chris Griscom's knowings of Death and Samadhi become richer in these times of planetary change. Chris addresses AIDS and illness and offers exercises which allow you to tap into your own ecstatic consciousness. $20 (not available in PAL)

Windows to the Sky, Part One: Light Institute Exercises with Chris Griscom These inspirational presentations are accompanied by exercises to enhance consciousness. Includes teachings about the Emotional Body, the Higher Self, the Inner Child, "The Dance of Relationship," and "The Cosmic Force of Sexuality." $30 (PAL $40)

Windows to the Sky, Part Two: Connecting with Invisible Worlds Chris explains our global involvement with the three major diseases of the decade: AIDS, cancer, and radiation. With the students of the Nizhoni School of Global Consciousness, she shows how to increase personal frequencies. Chris clarifies the influence of extra-terrestrials and communication with these and other sentient beings. $30 (PAL $40)

══ *Audio Tapes* ══

The Creative Self "No one has more power to imprint the world than the truly creative person." $15

The Dance of Relationship/La Danza de las Relaciones "How deeply we can merge with other souls depends on the realization of our own wholeness." Also available in Spanish. $15

Death and Samadhi "... reach across the veil into the unmanifest and pull in the recognition that allows us to be the master." $15

Desert Trilogy A set of three individual cassettes, each on a separate topic: "Healing," "Sexuality," and "Radiation" $20

Knowings Taken from Chris' Tuesday evening talks at The Light Institute, each tape is a wealth of information on current subjects. $15 each

Sense of Abundance "Never in human history have we been more ready to manifest all of our needs ... and never in human history have we thought that we needed so much." $15

Transcending Adversity "It's about expanding our perception so we can find the purpose in what is so seemingly adverse to us." $15